RESPONSIBLE TEST USE

CASE STUDIES FOR ASSESSING HUMAN BEHAVIOR

Lorraine D. Eyde
Gary J. Robertson
Samuel E. Krug
Kevin L. Moreland
Alan G. Robertson
Cynthia M. Shewan
Patti L. Harrison
Bruce E. Porch
Allen L. Hammer
Ernest S. Primoff

TEST USER TRAINING WORK GROUP OF THE JOINT COMMITTEE ON TESTING PRACTICES

Sponsored by American Counseling Association
American Psychological Association
American Speech-Language-Hearing Association
National Association of School Psychologists

American Psychological Association   Washington, DC

First printing July 1993
Second printing July 1994

Published by
American Psychological Association
750 First Street, NE
Washington, DC 20002

Copies may be ordered from
APA Order Department
P.O. Box 2710
Hyattsville, MD 20784

In the United Kingdom and Europe, copies may be ordered from
American Psychological Association
3 Henrietta Street
Covent Garden
London WC2E 8LU
England

Typeset in Trump Mediaeval and Optima by Easton Publishing Services, Inc., Easton, MD

Printer: Data Reproductions Corporation, Rochester Hills, MI
Cover designer: Berg Design, Albany, NY
Technical/production editor: Valerie Montenegro

The following citation for reference entries is recommended:

Eyde, L. D., Robertson, G. J., Krug, S. E., Moreland, K. L., Robertson, A. G., Shewan, C. M., Harrison, P. L., Porch, B. E., Hammer, A. L., & Primoff, E. S. (1993). *Responsible test use: Case studies for assessing human behavior*. Washington, DC: American Psychological Association.

Society for Industrial and Organizational Psychology, Inc. (SIOP) has generously granted permission to adapt material from *Casebook on Ethics and Standards for the Practice of Psychology in Organizations*, edited by R. L. Lowman. Copyright 1985 by SIOP.

Library of Congress Cataloging-in-Publication Data

Responsible test use: case studies for assessing human behavior/Lorraine D.
    Eyde . . . [et al.], Test User Training Work Group of the Joint Committee
    on Testing Practices; sponsored by American Counseling Association . . .
    [et al.].
        p.   cm.
    Includes bibliographical references and index.
    ISBN 1-55798-203-1 (pbk.; acid-free paper)
    1. Psychological tests.   2. Educational tests and measurements.
3. Behavioral assessment.   4. Psychological tests—Interpretation—Case
studies.   5. Educational tests and measurements—Interpretation—Case
studies.   6. Behavioral assessment—Case studies.   I. Eyde, Lorraine
D.   II. Joint Committee on Testing Practices. Test User Training Work
Group.   III. American Counseling Association.
BF176.R475   1993
153.9'3'076—dc20   93-1786
                                                              CIP

British Library Cataloguing-in-Publication Data
A CIP record is available from the British Library.

Printed in the United States of America

To Anne Anastasi, in recognition of her sustained effort to promote quality assurance in testing

CONTENTS

AUTHORS

Lorraine D. Eyde, U.S. Office of Personnel Management, Office of Personnel Research and Development, Washington, DC

Gary J. Robertson, American Guidance Service, Circle Pines, MN

Samuel E. Krug, MetriTech, Inc., Champaign, IL

Kevin L. Moreland, Fordham University, Bronx, New York

Alan G. Robertson (Retired), New York State Education Department, Office of Research and Evaluation, Albany, NY

Cynthia M. Shewan, American Speech-Language-Hearing Association, Rockville, MD[1]

Patti L. Harrison, University of Alabama, Tuscaloosa, AL

Bruce E. Porch, University of New Mexico, Albuquerque, NM

Allen L. Hammer, Consulting Psychologists Press, Palo Alto, CA

Ernest S. Primoff (Retired), U.S. Office of Personnel Management, Office of Personnel Research and Development, Washington, DC

The views expressed are those of the authors and do not necessarily reflect those of their employers or the sponsoring organizations.

[1]Cynthia Shewan is now with the American Physical Therapy Association, Alexandria, VA.

FOREWORD

Psychological and educational tests are a fundamental tool of many professionals. This is certainly true for professionals in the organizations sponsoring this casebook: the American Counseling Association, the American Psychological Association (APA), the American Speech-Language-Hearing Association, and the National Association of School Psychologists. Yet a persistent and troublesome problem in educational and psychological measurement has been the misuse of test data. This is generally not due to any intentional misinterpretation. Individuals in the organizations sponsoring this casebook are professionals who wish to use data wisely to help their constituents and other test users. Unfortunately, they frequently are unable to do so because of inadequate training in testing. *Responsible Test Use: Case Studies for Assessing Human Behavior* is an important publication because, if used widely, it should assist greatly in training professionals to use tests wisely.

Three outstanding features of this casebook are its broad and empirically based coverage of various factors in test use, its interdisciplinary approach with respect to settings and applications, and its thorough and user-friendly organization. Each of these outstanding features is explained briefly in the following paragraph.

The casebook was developed through an initial empirically based method for evaluating test users' competencies. Eighty-six specific elements and seven broad factors were identified that represent common problems in test use. These were used as the basis for soliciting 78 real-life cases from a variety of sources illustrating both proper and improper use of tests. The cases come from seven different settings or applications ranging from Counseling/Training to Speech-Language-Hearing. The organization of the casebook is by classification of case studies according to their natural sequence in the testing process. However, four alternative classification schemes are offered in the appendixes, and there is a worksheet for cross-referencing the cases to textbooks. Clearly the authors of this casebook have gone to extensive efforts to make it very user-friendly.

The case studies reported in this book demonstrate that there are numerous ways to misuse test data. The misuse of test data can result in increased errors such as misclassifications and misdiagnoses. These errors can result in considerable harm and be very costly to the individuals affected. Test misuse also is costly to all of society. If individuals receive psychological or educational treatments not needed, or do not receive needed treatments, the well-being of our society as a whole is affected. Finally, test misuse reflects poorly on the professional organizations whose members misuse data and casts both those professions and testing experts in a poor light.

The policy implication is clear. We must devote more resources to improving the ability of professionals to use test data wisely. This casebook is a very good example of a product that should facilitate improved test use. I am hopeful that it will be widely used—both as a supplement to textbooks by instructors and students in formal training/instruction settings, and by individual professionals in self-study.

The completion of a project of this size and quality is a difficult and time-consuming undertaking. Many individuals deserve much praise for their efforts. Certainly the 10 authors have worked long and hard on this project. However, countless others have contributed their time and talents by providing responses to the original survey, by providing cases, and by editing others' cases. While we owe all these individuals our thanks, it seems appropriate to especially thank the Executive Committee of the Test User Training Work Group: Lorraine D. Eyde, Gary J. Robertson, and Samuel E. Krug. They would be the first to thank all their hard-working colleagues. But the overall coordination and much of the writing was done by this executive committee, and they are particularly deserving of our thanks.

I commend this very important, high-quality casebook to all those who use educational and psychological test data. Studying it should make you a more competent professional—a goal to which we all should aspire.

WILLIAM A. MEHRENS
Professor
Michigan State University

ACKNOWLEDGMENTS

We are indebted to a great number of people who have helped in the various phases of this effort. We thank the Science Directorate of the American Psychological Association and its Committee on Psychological Tests and Assessment for the support provided for this project. We are grateful for the assistance provided by Wayne J. Camara and Dianne C. Brown and especially recognize the contributions of Sandra A. Yuen, Lynn T. Doty, and Dianne Schneider. We particularly thank Jan Flemino (American Guidance Service) for assisting our group. Our group thanks the Co-Chairs of the Joint Committee on Testing Practices (John J. Fremer and Jo-Ida Hansen) for encouraging the development of the casebook. This interdisciplinary effort would not have been possible without the support of Ted Remley and Nancy Pinson-Millburn (American Counseling Association), Frederick T. Spahr and Sharon C. Goldsmith (American Speech-Language-Hearing Association), and Richard Yep (National Association of School Psychologists). We appreciate the contributions of Anne Anastasi, Lee J. Cronbach, Janet E. Wall, Mary K. Schratz, Alice L. Palubinskas, Douglas K. Smith, Gerald S. Hanna, Ralph A. Alexander, Karen T. Carey, Joanne M. Lenke, Craig Linebaugh, Jane Faggen, Bruce R. Fretz, Georgiana Shick Tryon, Charles G. Eberly, and Hedwig Teglasi. We are grateful for Judy Nemes' probing questions, which resulted in improvements in our manuscript. We thank the contributors of critical incidents (appendix A) and the reviewers of cases and the casebook (appendix B).

LORRAINE D. EYDE

I

INTRODUCTION

1 DEVELOPMENT OF THE CASEBOOK

For more than four decades, professional associations have been concerned about test user competence (e.g., American Psychological Association [APA], 1950). During this time, test use has substantially increased, as has the number of test critics (see, e.g., Carter, 1965; National Commission on Testing and Public Policy, 1990). The testing function has been carried out increasingly by a variety of professionals in educational, counseling, employment, and mental health settings where test results may adversely affect the lives of test takers (Carter, 1965; Eyde, Moreland, Robertson, Primoff, & Most, 1988). As a result, professional associations have focused on promoting professional competence through the development of ethical principles and enforcement procedures (see American Speech-Language-Hearing Association [ASHA], 1991). Several professional associations have formal ethical principles that outline requirements for competent test use (American Association for Counseling and Development [AACD],[1] 1988; American Association of State Psychology Boards, 1991; APA, 1992a; Association for Psychological Type [APT], Undated a; National Association of School Psychologists [NASP], 1992a).

TEST USE GUIDELINES

In addition to ethical principles, professional associations and testing organizations have issued a large number of guidelines, for educational purposes, to promote proper test use. (See, e.g., AACD, 1989; American Federation of Teachers, National Council on Measurement in Education [NCME], & National Education Association, 1990; APA, 1992b; APT, Undated b; College Board, 1988; Costello & Weiss, 1984; Educational Testing Service [ETS], 1987, 1988, 1989; Joint Committee on Testing Practices [JCTP], 1988; Society for Industrial and Organizational Psychology, 1987; *Standards*, 1985).

Furthermore, guidelines for the delivery of services, which include assessment, have been developed (APA, 1987b; NASP, 1992b; Office of Ethnic Minority Affairs, 1990).

TEXTBOOKS

Testing textbooks have also grown in number. Since 1963, 67 texts dealing with tests and measurements and specialty testing have been published. Of these, 86% have appeared since 1979 (see appendix C). Test users have numerous other educational resources available (e.g., in the counseling field, see Mehrens & Lehmann, 1985; Rawlins & Eberly, 1991; Tinsley & Bradley, 1986). Evaluations of the impact of educational materials are rare. However, Elmore, Ekstrom, and Diamond (in press) conducted a survey of school counselors and found that good test interpretation practice was associated with educational variables such as preservice and inservice training, confidence in knowledge of measurement concepts, and familiarity with test use guidelines.

CONFERENCES

Numerous conferences have dealt with ways of encouraging good testing practices (APA, 1981; Anastasi, 1989a; Cordes, 1984; Eyde, Green, & Jackson, 1984). The 1981 APA Conference on Testing, Assessment, and Public Policy recommended developing methods for measuring test user competence and a casebook of good and bad testing practices. In 1984, an APA-sponsored test publishers' meeting called for a project on test user qualifi-

---

[1] The American Counseling Association (ACA) was formerly the American Association for Counseling and Development.

cations and led to the founding of the JCTP,[2] an interdisciplinary group promoting quality assurance in testing.

TEST USER QUALIFICATIONS WORKING GROUP

This casebook grew out of the work of two committees of the JCTP: the Test User Qualifications Working Group (TUQWoG) and its successor group, the Test User Training Work Group (TUTWoG). TUQWoG (Eyde, Moreland, et al., 1988; Eyde & Primoff, 1992; Robertson, 1992) identified the knowledges, skills, abilities, and other personal characteristics required for responsible use of 76 commercially published tests sold to individual test purchasers. By applying two empirical job analysis methods (Flanagan, 1954; Primoff, 1975; Primoff & Eyde, 1988), TUQWoG developed an empirical method for evaluating test user competencies and test purchaser forms for use by test publishers in screening persons seeking to buy tests. By applying Primoff's job element method to an extensive database of "critical incidents" of test misuse contributed by 62 testing professionals, TUQWoG (Eyde, Moreland, et al., 1988) found 86 specific elements (appendix E) and seven broad factors that represented problems commonly encountered across many different kinds of tests and testing situations.[3] Anne Anastasi (1989a), who served as an informal consultant to TUQWoG, was one of the first persons to recognize the educational potential of TUQWoG's critical incidents.

CASE DEVELOPMENT

After TUQWoG completed its work, TUTWoG was established under the JCTP. This new group made plans to apply the database of critical incidents, elements, and factors of test misuse to the development of an interdisciplinary casebook, to be sponsored by the ACA, the APA, ASHA, and NASP. The casebook was designed for use in introductory graduate courses in tests and measurements as well as for use in inservice and other continuing education activities. The book may also be used by practitioners as a reference book for self-study. Details about the preparation of the casebook and sources are provided in appendix F.

COMPREHENSIVE CASE COVERAGE

In order to develop a casebook relevant to the training and education needs of the sponsoring organizations, we needed to extend the content coverage of the cases beyond the original TUQWoG database. Test coverage was expanded to include college admissions tests and licensing examinations. A major effort was launched to collect and assemble a comprehensive set of critical incidents by tapping the TUQWoG database and contacting members of the testing community for new cases. We also published articles in newsletters to solicit specific kinds of cases ("Contributors Sought," 1990; "Examples of Test Misuse Needed," 1991; "Test Misuse: A Target of Concern," 1990; "Test User Training Work Group Formed," 1990; "Test User Training Work Group Needs Examples of Test Misuse," 1991). The newsletter articles called attention to the need for cases dealing with the following areas: kindergarten students; cross-cultural testing of adults; neuropsychology; teacher

---

[2]The JCTP is sponsored by the ACA, the APA, ASHA, the NCME, and NASP. The JCTP represents a collaborative effort between test publishers and professional associations to promote quality assurance in testing. The JCTP originally set up two working groups: TUQWoG and a second group to develop a Code of Fair Testing Practices in Education (Fremer, Diamond, & Camara, 1989). Once their work was completed, these two groups were sunsetted and two new groups formed: TUTWoG and the Understanding Testing Work Group.

[3]For comments on the projects, see Anastasi, 1988, 1989a, 1989b, 1992a, 1992b, 1993; Bond, Camara, and VandenBos 1989; Cohen, Swerdlik, and Smith, 1992; Cronbach, 1990; Elmore, Ekstrom, and Diamond, in press; Jenkinson, 1991; Lambert, 1991; Rawlins and Eberly, 1991; and Thorndike, Cunningham, Thorndike, and Hagen, 1991.

use of tests in the classroom; college admissions selection (SAT and ACT); testing of women, minorities, and older persons; and storing of test information in files and length of time appropriate for its use.

Fifty testing professionals (see appendix A) contributed the critical incidents used in the casebook by completing the form in appendix G. To round out the collection, cases from previously published casebooks and other publications were adapted (APA, 1984; APA, 1987a; Eyde & Quaintance, 1988; Lowman, 1985; Pennock-Román, 1988). This casebook contains 78 cases that are related to the factors and elements of test misuse from the 1988 study (Eyde, Moreland, et al., 1988). Nine cases were dropped because they failed to meet the criteria listed in appendix F.

ACTUAL BEHAVIOR DESCRIBED

The cases are based on real-life testing situations with some details changed to protect the identity of individuals and organizations. Cases deal with professional interpretation of test results to individuals and with interpretations of test results aggregated for individuals in organizations. Although reviewers found some cases unbelievable, the facts were drawn from real situations. Some cases came from published ethics casebooks. Others were newly submitted cases from reliable sources. The cases vary in the level of detail presented and in their complexity, reflecting the incidents submitted to us. Although most cases involve test misuse, some cases exemplifying responsible test use were also included. (For more information on how cases were obtained, see appendix F.)

Despite our extensive solicitation of cases, the casebook does not cover all possible types of test misuse. Nor are the studies necessarily exhaustive in their coverage of all the possible ramifications of a particular instance of test misuse. The casebook reflects the nature of critical incidents sent to us and cases from published sources. Cases are not intended to reflect typical testing practice or indicate the frequency of test misuse. The casebook includes references to actual published tests but neither endorses nor indicts specific tests. The book was not designed to deal with the appropriateness of using a particular test for certain purposes.

CASEBOOK CAVEATS

The casebook reflects the professional judgment of those who submitted the cases, thoughtful reviewers who prepared more than 890 reviews, and members of the TUTWoG. It is not:

- an ethics casebook (different professional associations have different formal ethical principles and adjudication procedures in dealing with test misuse)
- the policy of any of the sponsoring organizations
- designed *specifically* for use in training for compliance with any of the previously mentioned testing standards
- designed for use as a litigation tool.

In summary, this casebook was designed to emphasize important areas for professional training, raise questions about test use, instruct students in proper use, and stimulate students and teachers to explore issues beyond the boundaries of specific cases. Cases may be interpreted in numerous ways. The casebook is designed to encourage testing professionals to expand the opportunities of their clients, rather than restrict opportunities. Test misuse, where it exists, can be overcome. This casebook is based on the assumption that proper test use requires important knowledges, skills, abilities, and other personal characteristics that can be learned through formal education or training or by self-instruction.

2 How to Use the Casebook

The casebook was developed to extend the application of principles of proper test interpretation and use learned in the classroom to the real world, where tests are used daily in a variety of settings to make vital decisions affecting the lives of individuals. Thus, the goal of the Test User Training Work Group (TUTWoG) was to provide a collection of case studies based on actual incidents of proper and improper test use that could be used to supplement the basic textbooks used in testing and assessment courses. Much of the material taught in introductory measurement courses is, of necessity, abstract and often linked rather indirectly to the actual use of tests in applied settings. The casebook gives students and instructors that link to the real world of test use. Its organization facilitates its use in both traditional academic settings as well as in training programs, workshops on test interpretation and use, and in various types of continuing education courses. The casebook will also help individuals engaged in self-study improve their use and interpretation of tests. Practitioners will find the various case studies of value for reviewing basic principles of test use as well as extending their understanding of testing in applied settings. These cases may be used also by state licensing boards in examining licensure candidates for responsible test use.

The casebook's major emphasis is on the application of basic principles of sound test selection, use, and interpretation across seven settings or areas of application within which tests are used: Counseling/Training, Education, Employment, General, Mental Health, Neuropsychology, and Speech-Language-Hearing. Flexibility and ease of use in a variety of instructional settings have remained guiding principles in developing and organizing the casebook.

ORGANIZATION

The 78 case studies that illustrate both proper and improper use of tests constitute the major portion of the casebook. The incidents described in four cases (3, 11, 22, 25) emphasize, for the most part, good testing practices. One case (67), which deals with a controversial issue, offers the pros and cons of the practice in the analysis. The remaining cases concentrate on correcting improper test use. In addition, a series of appendixes provide supplementary reference information and additional organizational schemes designed to enhance the utility of the casebook for instructors, students, and other users. An explanation of the organization and content of major sections of the casebook follows.

CLASSIFICATION OF CASE STUDIES

The case studies are grouped into sections that reflect a natural sequence of events in the testing process: issues of professional training, test selection, test administration and scoring, interpretation, reporting to clients, and administrative and organizational policy issues. Many instructors will find that this organizational scheme reflects a logical sequence in which students acquire basic understandings of measurement concepts. Instructors will find, however, that the case studies can be assigned in any order, depending upon the arrangement of topics in the course syllabus. A procedure for linking the case studies to textbooks and instructional topics is explained in the section Cross-Referencing Cases to Textbooks and the Course Syllabus. Instructors who prefer alternative organization schemes, by setting or application, by type of test, or by the Test User Qualifications Working Group (TUQWoG) factors or elements, for example, will find the appendixes helpful in facilitating such use.

ALTERNATIVE CLASSIFICATION SCHEMES

In order to maximize the utility of the casebook, three alternative classification schemes are offered in the appendixes: by the setting and application in which the incident occurred (appendix J), by the empirically developed elements of competent test use (appendix K), and by the research-based factors of proper test use (appendix L). A fourth alternative is provided by general type of test in the section Cross-Referencing Cases to Textbooks and the Course Syllabus. A brief description of each of these alternative classification schemes follows.

Classification by Setting and Applications

Appendix J classifies the 78 case studies by seven settings in which tests are used: Counseling/Training, Education, Employment, General, Mental Health, Neuropsychology, and Speech-Language-Hearing. Some instructors may find a need to reference the case studies by the setting in which the incident occurred. For example, an instructor teaching an educational measurement course may want to locate those case studies that reflect educational concerns. Similarly, an instructor of an industrial–organizational psychology course may need to locate cases that take place in employment settings. Appendix J facilitates finding such information quickly. However, early in its research, TUTWoG investigated the relationship between test misuse and setting. Results showed that the various types of test misuse generalize across settings. Thus, readers who focus exclusively or too narrowly on setting may miss cases that have important implications for their work.

Classification by the Elements of Competent Test Use

Appendix K classifies the 78 case studies by the 86 elements of competent test use used as a basis for the work conducted by TUTWoG. The case studies appearing in the casebook were derived principally from 62 critical incidents of test misuse supplied by testing experts contacted by TUQWoG in its research on the development of improved test purchaser qualification procedures (Eyde, Moreland et al., 1988). Additional critical incidents were obtained by TUTWoG in order to extend coverage across other types of tests and to identify instances of exemplary test use. From the 62 critical incidents collected by TUQWoG, Primoff (1975) used Job Element methodology to abstract the 86 elements of competent test use listed in appendix E. These elements represent knowledges, skills, abilities, and other personal characteristics related to proper test use (Eyde, Moreland et al., 1988, pp. 26, 27). A sampling of 24 of the 86 elements is shown in the right-hand column of Exhibit 1. Instructors may find it useful to reference the cases to specific elements of proper test use if certain of the elements are receiving special emphasis in course content.

Classification by the Factors of Proper Test Use

Appendix L classifies cases by seven broad factors of proper test use that underlie the 86 elements (Eyde, Moreland et al., 1988). The original TUQWoG database consisted of 487 ratings of published tests on the 86 elements of competent test use. The ratings were supplied by 200 experts in the mid-1980s. Principal-axes factor analysis with varimax rotation was used to identify seven underlying dimensions of proper test use. These seven factors of proper test use together with the elements of competent test use loaded highest on each are shown in the left-hand column of Exhibit 1 (Eyde, Moreland et al., 1988). A brief definition of each factor is also provided to help clarify its meaning.

Students and instructors may find the definitions of the factors shown in Exhibit 1 useful in gaining more insight into the meaning of the factors as these relate to the content of measurement courses. Some instructors may wish to emphasize the factors as part of the instructional process. Cross-referencing the cases by the factors facilitates the use of the cases as these relate to the factors.

Exhibit 1. Abridged Elements of Competent Test Use Loading Highest on Seven Factors of Proper Test Use

Factor	Elements
1. Comprehensive Assessment Following up testing to get pertinent personal history data to integrate with test scores to enhance accuracy of interpretation.	23. Psychosocial history. 35. Considering patient's state. 37. Teaching research evidence and test limitations. 45. Choice of test to sample relevant behaviors. 77. Follow-up with psychosocial history. 79. Use of tests to generate hypotheses. 82. Proper reporting of clinical observations during testing.
2. Proper Test Use Accepting the responsibility for competent use of the test; exercising appropriate quality control procedures over all aspects of test use.	1. Acceptance of responsibility for competent use of the test. 7. Refraining from helping a favored person earn a good score. 8. Appropriate training and quality control over operations for all users of tests and test results.
3. Psychometric Knowledge Knowing and using correctly basic statistical principles of measurement (e.g., standard error of measurement, reliability, validity).	20. Considering errors of measurement of a test score. 32. Considering the standard error of measurement. 44. Understanding the standard error of measurement.
4. Maintaining Integrity of Test Results Correctly applying psychometric principles to the actual interpretation of test results; understanding the limitations of test scores.	39. Advising administrators about limitations of grade equivalent scores and percentile ranks for specific situations. 49. Making clear that absolute cut-off scores are questionable because they ignore measurement error.
5. Accuracy of Scoring Ensuring that all aspects of test scoring (e.g., recording, checking, correct reading of tables) are performed correctly.	55. Avoiding errors in scoring and recording. 56. Using checks on scoring accuracy. 57. Checking frequently during scoring to catch lapses. 58. Following scoring directions.
6. Appropriate Use of Norms Understanding and using different types of norms correctly, particularly in employment settings.	31. Matching person to job on aptitude validities. 59. Not assuming that a norm for one job applies to a different job.
7. Interpretive Feedback to Clients Providing correct interpretations of test scores to test takers.	71. Willingness to give interpretation and guidance to test takers in counseling situations. 72. Ability to give interpretation and guidance to test takers in counseling situations. 73. Having enough staff to provide counseling.

Note. Adapted with permission from Eyde, Moreland, Robertson, Primoff, and Most (1988). Wording of elements has occasionally been abridged. For complete text of elements, see appendix E.

Classification by General Types of Tests

The section Cross-Referencing Cases to Textbooks and the Course Syllabus classifies cases by 12 generic test types: educational achievement, employment, group scholastic ability, hearing, individual intelligence, interest, multiple abilities, neuropsychological, personality, projective, readiness, and speech-language. Instructors will find this classification scheme helpful when cases pertaining to a particular type of test need to be located quickly.

Because the casebook was developed as a supplement to be used with a measurement textbook, the casebook authors made no attempt to teach the characteristics of either general types of tests or specific published tests. It was assumed that such information would be obtained from a textbook or from the study of a published test.

STRUCTURE OF THE CASE STUDIES

The following structure is used for each of the 78 case studies: Title, Setting/Application, Incident, Focus Questions, Analysis, Factor(s) Involved, and Element(s) Involved. Factors and elements are *listed in the order of importance* in each case. Following are descriptions of each of these case study components:

Setting and Applications

As previously explained, each case originally occurred in one of seven settings or applications: Counseling/Training, Education, Employment, General, Mental Health, Neuropsychology, and Speech-Language-Hearing.

Incident

This section describes the instance of proper or improper test use together with pertinent details. Instructors may want to have the students role play the major roles of persons in the cases to better understand their motivations and explore other consequences that may not be fully explored within the written description.

Focus Questions

These questions were developed to stimulate thought and discussion of the most important aspects of the case. The questions presented are by no means the only ones that could be asked to focus students and other readers on the most pertinent aspects of the case. For this reason, the questions are, by design, very broad and general in nature. Instructors, in particular, are encouraged to add their own questions as needed. Certain obvious questions that could be used for almost every case are not listed. Examples of these are: What was the purpose of testing? What are the consequences of the particular course of action taken? Are there other elements (or factors) of proper test use in addition to those listed that also apply to the case?

Analysis

The analysis presents a discussion of the major points that need to be taken into account. The analysis covers most points raised by the Focus Questions, although no systematic attempt was made to answer every Focus Question. It must be emphasized, however, that there are usually no simple right or wrong answers. The analysis is not intended to be an exhaustive treatment of all aspects of the case. Readers will undoubtedly find other pertinent points that need to be stressed.

Factor(s) Involved

One or more of the seven factors of proper test use discussed previously and shown in Exhibit 1 are listed in order of their relevance to the case. Instructors who are emphasizing the factors in course work will find this reference helpful. Discussion of the case may also be expanded to include a discussion of the relationship of the incident to the factor(s). Such discussions can contribute to a richer understanding of the factors of proper test use. If additional factors from the list of seven shown in Exhibit 1 and appendix L seem to apply to a particular case, these may be added if there is sufficient justification for their inclusion.

Element(s) Involved

One or more of the 86 elements of competent test use discussed previously and shown in appendix E are listed in order of their relevance to the case. Instructors who are emphasizing the elements in course work will find this listing helpful. Discussion of the case may also be expanded to include a discussion of the relationship of the element(s) to the incident. Such discussions can contribute greatly to an enhanced understanding of those fundamental aspects of competent test use that apply to a particular case. Appendix E contains the complete listing of elements listed in the cases. If additional elements from the list of 86 shown in appendix K seem to apply to a particular case, these may be added if there is sufficient justification for their inclusion.

Additional Instructional Suggestions

The case study format is particularly well suited to a variety of instructional uses. For example, instructors may prefer to have students read and discuss the Incident and Focus Questions before reading the Analysis section. The casebook format was designed to facilitate such use by placing the Incident and Focus Questions on one page and the Analysis, Factors, and Elements on a second page. (Blank space follows the Incident and Focus Questions for most cases and may be used by readers to record notes pertaining to the cases or Focus Questions.) Students may also be asked to determine the seven factors of proper test use and the elements of competent test use, with appropriate justification for their selection, before reviewing those listed at the end of a case. In class discussions, students may be asked to describe appropriate and inappropriate behaviors depicted in a case, with appropriate justification. The case studies may also be used to further the understanding of the ethical principles developed by a specific professional organization such as the American Psychological Association (APA), the American Counseling Association (ACA), the American Speech-Language-Hearing Association (ASHA), and the National Association of School Psychologists (NASP) by having students determine the ethical principles for the professional organization relevant to their area of study illustrated in a particular case. Certain of the case studies lend themselves well to the development of organizational policy statements to prevent the recurrence of various test misuses, and students may be asked to draft policy statements for discussion with class members. Use of the small group discussion format is especially recommended to enhance student learning from the case studies. It should be noted that the aforementioned activities recommended for students can also be used with individuals attending inservice workshops, continuing education courses, and other professionals who find the case study format useful.

CROSS-REFERENCING CASES TO TEXTBOOKS AND THE COURSE SYLLABUS

The authors of the casebook recognized early that one essential requirement for acceptance of the casebook by instructors and students was the ease of linking cases to textbook readings and course syllabus topics. The ideal scheme would provide the instructor with case studies linked to the particular textbook used in the course. Practical limitations such as rapid obsolescence due to the publication of new editions and new texts as well as casebook space limitations and the magnitude of effort required to index 67 textbooks all precluded the provision of such a listing. Instead, a system was devised that identified a common core of topics covered in a representative sample of the textbooks listed in appendix C. These core content topics represent such fundamental domains of knowledge that they can be expected to remain relatively invariant across textbooks as well as across successive editions of the same textbook, thereby avoiding the problem of becoming obsolete when a textbook is revised. The 78 cases were then classified according to this core list. Exhibit 2 shows the listing of core content topics. Using this core list, it then becomes possible for

Exhibit 2. Worksheet for Cross-Referencing Cases to Textbooks

Course _____ Instructor _____

Textbook _____ Publisher _____

Core Content Topic	Case Studies (by Number)	Textbook Chapter	Pages
Test Selection/Choice of Assessment Procedure	1, 4, 5, 11, 14, 17, 18, 19, 22, 27, 28, 29, 30, 31, 32, 33, 35, 36, 40, 44, 46, 49, 50, 51, 52, 53, 54, 55, 57, 59, 60, 68, 69, 70, 71, 72, 73, 75, 77, 78		
Test Administration/Scoring	1, 2, 4, 6, 9, 12, 13, 15, 17, 18, 19, 20, 21, 25, 26, 33, 34, 35, 36, 37, 38, 39, 40, 41, 42, 43, 44, 46, 49, 57, 60, 62, 66, 67, 72, 73, 74, 75, 76		
PSYCHOMETRICS			
Descriptive Statistics	14, 30, 69, 71, 73		
Types and Uses of Norms	4, 11, 14, 16, 24, 27, 29, 30, 34, 35, 36, 40, 44, 45, 46, 47, 52, 53, 57, 60, 61, 63, 69, 71, 72, 73, 74, 76		
Reliability	45, 47, 54, 73, 75		
Validity	2, 4, 11, 16, 21, 26, 27, 28, 29, 36, 38, 40, 41, 42, 43, 47, 49, 50, 55, 56, 57, 59, 60, 69, 71, 73, 75, 77, 78		
TYPES OF TESTS			
Educational Achievement	24, 28, 44, 45, 52, 54, 60, 69, 72, 76		
Employment	2, 6, 27, 33, 39, 42, 48, 55, 68, 77		
Group Scholastic Ability	43, 54, 56, 71, 74, 78		
Hearing	20, 38, 53, 60		
Individual Intelligence	5, 20, 35, 36, 46, 51, 53, 55, 58		
Interest	10, 50, 63, 67		
Multiple Abilities	34, 47, 50, 61, 63		
Neuropsychological	5, 16, 17, 18, 19, 31, 32, 40, 46, 58, 59		
Personality	1, 7, 11, 21, 22, 23, 48, 49, 57, 58, 62, 64, 65, 66, 67, 68, 70		
Projective	3, 5, 12, 13, 15, 64		
Readiness	30		
Speech/Language	14, 29, 30, 37, 53, 73, 75		

(*continues on next page*)

(Exhibit 2—*continued from previous page*)

Core Content Topic	Case Studies (by Number)	Textbook Chapter	Pages
SPECIAL APPLICATIONS			
Testing Special Populations	28, 36, 76		
Gender	2, 47, 61		
Individuals with Disabilities	20, 25, 34, 36, 39, 40, 41, 42, 43, 53, 59, 60, 73, 75		
Minorities	2, 4, 14, 26, 30, 35, 56, 57, 69		
Reasonable Accommodations/ Modifications	20, 34, 39, 40, 41, 42, 43, 60		
Age Groups			
Preschool (0–5 years)	14, 29, 30, 53, 75		
School (6–18 years)	3, 4, 9, 12, 16, 20, 24, 25, 26, 35, 43, 44, 45, 47, 50, 51, 52, 53, 54, 56, 60, 61, 63, 69, 72, 73, 74, 76		
College (19–22 years)	1, 10, 15, 28, 49, 50, 74, 78		
Adult (23–64 years)	2, 5, 6, 7, 11, 17, 18, 21, 22, 23, 27, 28, 31, 32, 33, 34, 36, 39, 40, 41, 42, 48, 49, 55, 57, 58, 59, 62, 64, 65, 66, 67, 70, 71, 77		
Elderly (65 + years)	46		
Factors Influencing Test Results	4, 6, 9, 17, 20, 21, 25, 26, 33, 34, 35, 36, 37, 40, 41, 42, 43, 44, 46, 53, 54, 57, 58, 59, 60, 61, 62, 66, 69, 70, 71, 72, 73, 74, 75, 76, 78		
Test Translations	4, 35, 40, 57		
Legal/Ethical Considerations	1, 2, 3, 4, 5, 6, 7, 8, 9, 10, 12, 13, 15, 16, 18, 20, 23, 24, 26, 27, 39, 40, 41, 42, 43, 48, 49, 51, 53, 55, 56, 57, 62, 63, 64, 65, 66, 67, 68, 69, 72, 74, 76, 77		
Public Reporting of Test Results	14, 24, 27, 69, 74, 76		
MISCELLANEOUS TOPICS			
Use of Test Records	6, 30, 35, 44, 51		
Diagnostic Evaluation/ Interpretation	4, 5, 14, 18, 19, 29, 30, 31, 32, 35, 36, 37, 40, 45, 46, 48, 49, 50, 51, 53, 58, 59		
Planning Interventions	9, 14, 17, 18, 35, 45, 48, 60		
Psychological Screening	7, 11, 57		

an instructor to match the content area to chapters or relevant pages of both the course syllabus and the particular textbook used in the course.

Exhibit 2, Worksheet for Cross-Referencing Cases to Textbooks, provides a convenient device for instructors to use to establish the basic linkage between the course textbook and the casebook case studies. In the column headed Textbook Reference, list the relevant chapter(s) and pages in the textbook used. Appropriate cases may then be easily assigned when the particular topics listed are covered in the course. The column headed Case Studies (by Number) contains a listing of all cases applicable to a particular core content topic. Students can easily circle the numbers of the cases assigned, or instructors may circle assigned cases, photocopy the worksheet, and distribute it as part of the course syllabus.

Considerable latitude was used to assign cases to core content topics. For any specific core content topic, a variety of cases will be found ranging from those whose central problem is related to that core content topic to others where there is only minimal relevance. Such a scheme was felt to be of greatest potential use to instructors who will want to choose specific cases to assign as readings in view of the type of course, the emphasis placed on the various core content topics, and the characteristics of the students.

Appendix D contains a duplicate of the worksheet shown in Exhibit 2. Instructors may photocopy this worksheet in order to avoid mutilating the casebook. We welcome receiving completed worksheets for various textbooks and will serve as a clearinghouse so that these may be shared with users of the casebook who request cases linked to a particular textbook. Textbook authors may also wish to include completed worksheets, cross-referenced for use with their texts, in their instructor's manuals.

The textbook cross-referencing system offered is only one of several possible systems that might be devised. Casebook users who devise useful alternative schemes are encouraged to forward these to us[1] so that they may be shared with the casebook authors and users, who may find them helpful. These submissions will also assist the authors in preparing possible casebook supplements or future editions.

A SPECIAL REQUEST TO CASEBOOK USERS

After you have used the casebook and can evaluate its organization and content, please complete the User Comment sheet shown in appendix H and forward it to Dr. Eyde at the address noted so that future editions of the casebook may be improved. The authors and publisher welcome comments and suggestions for improvement from all types of users—students, instructors, and others who have used the casebook. Casebook users are encouraged to submit critical incidents of good or poor test use. The Critical Incident Report form in Appendix I may be photocopied and used for this purpose.

---

[1] Write Lorraine D. Eyde, PhD, % Science Directorate, American Psychological Association, 750 First Street NE, Washington, DC 20002-4242.

II
CASES

Section 1 ———————————.

Training: General

1 Personality Evaluation in a Scholarship Program

Mental Health

Incident

Each year, a small liberal arts college offered incoming students several awards that covered all tuition and expenses for 4 years of undergraduate study. In recent years, the academic careers of two students who won these awards were disrupted by emotional difficulties so severe that they were unable to finish their undergraduate programs. To avoid future failures, the college decided to add emotional stability to its criteria for awarding these scholarships. Because its resources were limited, the college hired a psychologist to train two nurses from the college infirmary staff to administer and interpret a battery of personality tests. These nurses had no prior training in psychological assessment. The training consisted of a brief introduction to the Minnesota Multiphasic Personality Inventory (MMPI) and instructions in its administration and scoring. Staff members learned that a T score above 70 on scales 1, 2, 3, 6, 7, or 8 was sufficient to disqualify a candidate because of emotional instability. Completed answer sheets and profiles were to be retained by the infirmary staff in locked files. Only a pass/fail decision was to be noted in the applicant's record. The psychologist provided supplies of test materials sufficient for several years of operation.

One unsuccessful applicant told his parents that he had taken personality tests. The parents learned that infirmary staff had administered the tests and discovered the nature of their training. Subsequently, they brought an ethics charge against the psychologist who had trained the two nurses. In response to an inquiry by her profession's Ethics Committee, the psychologist replied that she had no idea her actions could have been construed as unethical. Besides the direct training she provided, the psychologist had given the nurses her office phone number and urged them to call if any difficulties arose. None had.

Focus Questions

What other methods could be used to determine the emotional stability of scholarship applicants?

How could the psychologist have better assured quality control of the procedures used by the nurses?

What type of training should be given to persons administering the MMPI?

Should the applicant's file include the MMPI test scores, or is a pass/fail judgment sufficient?

The psychologist involved had not considered all the implications and ramifications of such a sensitive, but unsupervised, testing program. Without adequate training in psychological assessment, the infirmary staff probably relied too inflexibly on the results of one test.

The psychologist made no provisions for considering contextual or situational factors in the interpretation of test results. The decision rule did not consider the evidence available in the validity scales of the MMPI. Nor did it provide an alternative evaluation procedure for an invalid test protocol. Unsuccessful candidates for the scholarship may have felt that they somehow "flunked" the psychological test.

The college's goal in seeking to identify able candidates who also have sufficient personal resources to complete an undergraduate program is reasonable. Considering the importance of the award, however, it seems unreasonable to place so much emphasis on a single test score. A better approach for the psychologist might have been to identify a member of the psychology faculty with background knowledge in personality theory, abnormal psychology, and testing that would have rendered his or her training program more effective. In addition, the psychologist would have needed to work with the college to develop a cost-effective and accurate method for further assessing those candidates with "suspect" MMPI results. Alternatively, the psychologist might have worked with the college to develop support systems within the college to make those pressures on students more manageable. Thus, the psychologist might have worked with the counseling staff, helped the school develop a peer counseling program, or provided other assistance that only an outside consultant can offer.

FACTORS
INVOLVED

2. Proper Test Use
1. Comprehensive Assessment

ELEMENTS
INVOLVED

2. Knowledge of professional ethics.
8. Providing appropriate training and quality control over operations for all users of tests and test results.
86. Refraining from reporting scores to administrators without adequate interpretation.
30. Resisting political pressures to shorten the planning, diagnostic, and interpretive process unduly.
23. Skill in taking a good history to integrate with test results.
22. Knowledge of the need for multiple sources of convergent data.

2 THE CARELESS PERSONNEL DIRECTOR

Employment

A personnel director wanted to develop a testing program that would help in the selection of employees for jobs requiring mechanical skills. She also wanted to ensure that these procedures would be defensible in case any complaints of discrimination based on sex or race were made to the Equal Employment Opportunity Commission.

The director examined several test publishers' catalogs and chose the Bennett Mechanical Comprehension Test. She purchased a supply of test booklets and answer sheets and instructed her secretary to administer tests to the applicants. The secretary had no prior training or experience that would qualify her for this task. She assumed that the test was self-administering and handed the test and answer sheet to applicants when they appeared. Also, she ignored the recommended time limit because "most applicants finish the test anyway."

Distributions of test scores were generated for protected and nonprotected classes, separately by gender. The midpoint of each distribution became the cut-off. The director believed that this would protect the company from any charges of discrimination.

Does the personnel director's review of available tests seem sufficient? What other sources could she have examined?

Why was the personnel director's determination of cut-off scores not defensible?

Failure to follow the recommended procedures for administration of the instrument makes interpretation of the test scores difficult, and sometimes impossible. The reliability, validity, and normative information provided in the test manual is gathered under standard administration conditions. It may not apply to nonstandard situations.

The determination of cut-off scores is always a sensitive issue. It must be done in ways that meet legitimate needs of the employer and comply with applicable law and professional standards. The 1991 Civil Rights Act, which forbids the use of race norming, makes the personnel director's use of separate cut-offs illegal.

If people were already employed in the position for which the testing program was developed, the personnel director might have studied the score distribution of incumbents in setting a less arbitrary cut score. Once the testing program was begun, follow-up of successful candidates would be desirable to check on the validity of both the test and the cut score.

FACTORS INVOLVED

2. Proper Test Use
6. Appropriate Use of Norms

ELEMENTS INVOLVED

1. Accepting responsibility for competent use of the test.
8. Providing appropriate training and quality control over operations for all users of tests and test results.
15. Restricting test administration to qualified personnel.
17. Knowledge of the test and its limitations.
61. Seeing that every examinee follows directions so that test scores are accurate.
63. Following timing instructions accurately, especially for short speeded tests.
65. Giving standard directions as prescribed.
64. Refraining from equating sex/race samples by adjusting norms to fit subsample results.

3 TESTS ARE NOT TOYS

Mental Health

INCIDENT

A toy manufacturing company particularly interested in painting and drawing materials invited a testing expert to develop a drawing test that could give parents "valuable information regarding the personality development of the child." The psychologist had been impressed by the amount of information that could be obtained through children's drawings, particularly when supplemented by a questionnaire that she had used in private practice for many years. Before signing a contract with the firm, however, she wished to be certain that such an arrangement with a commercial enterprise was proper and queried the ethics committee of her professional association as to whether the test could be placed in the hands of parents. The ethics committee objected to the plan to promote the test to parents, believing that they would not be able to use the test—as conceived by the psychologist and the toy company—properly. The testing expert did not execute the contract.

FOCUS QUESTION

Are there ways in which the psychologist could have assured that her drawing test would have been used appropriately by parents?

This is an example of appropriate action by a testing professional. The clinician was appropriately sensitive to the generally accepted wisdom that laypersons are not equipped to interpret projective tests. She checked with an appropriate professional body before contracting with the toy company, thereby avoiding actions that quite likely would have been deemed a violation of professional standards of good testing practice.

The untrained are at risk for making inappropriate decisions of all kinds based on misunderstanding of the test results. This danger is compounded when the test deals with individual differences that are unfamiliar to many (e.g., constructs from many personality theories); may well have negative connotations in the eyes of many people (e. g., introversion in modern western society); and the constructs are widely thought to be important to success in many areas of life.

Testing professionals, like the one in this case, should make sure that tests and test results are used only by those capable of using them properly. This does not mean restricting the use of tests to persons with specified credentials. It does mean that one must carefully specify the knowledges, skills, abilities, and other characteristics required to use a given test properly and be equally careful in making sure that proposed users possess those knowledges, skills, abilities, and other characteristics.

2. Proper Test Use
4. Integrity of Test Results

1. Accepting responsibility for competent use of the test.
8. Providing appropriate training and quality control over operations for all users of tests and test results.
15. Restricting test administration to qualified personnel.
17. Knowledge of the test and its limitations.
34. Considering whether the reason for giving a test locally meets the purpose for which the test was designed.

4 TEST MISUSE IN ASSESSING LIMITED ENGLISH PROFICIENT (LEP) CHILDREN

SETTING AND APPLICATIONS

Education

INCIDENT

Two Hispanic siblings of Puerto Rican descent whose primary language was Spanish and whose secondary language was English, a boy aged 9½ years and a girl aged 8 years, were referred from the local school system to a nearby child development clinic affiliated with a national hospital chain for evaluation and diagnosis of behavior problems in school. The children had been living in the United States for 2 years and had a normal developmental history according to school records, although there was no record of the parents having been interviewed. The school staff did not feel the children's problems stemmed from their LEP status or an inability to meet academic requirements.

A developmental pediatrician and a pediatric resident interviewed the children and administered the Peabody Picture Vocabulary Test–Revised (PPVT-R), the Slosson Oral Reading Test (SORT), the Bender Gestalt Test, and the Pediatric Elementary Examination. Neither physician had prior training or experience in assessing LEP children. A neighbor who served as their after-school baby-sitter served as translator when this was required to communicate the test directions, the items, or the children's responses.

The physicians' summary report identified significant deficits in both children, with the greatest impairment identified as language skills, particularly vocabulary and reading comprehension as measured by the PPVT-R and the SORT. The children were also said to have "great difficulty with sequencing tasks, and less delay with the visual and perceptual tasks." Based on the preceding assessment results, the older child was diagnosed as having a mixed specific developmental delay; moreover, it was observed that this condition, if combined with inappropriate classroom placement, could explain the child's behavior problems in the classroom. No specific diagnosis was given for the younger child other than noting that her language handicap "could be expected to adversely affect her academic performance and, thus, could result in behavior problems."

FOCUS QUESTIONS

What kinds of evidence should have been obtained as a starting point in evaluating these children?

What errors were made in test selection and interpretation?

What are the necessary examiner qualifications for assessing LEP children?

What mistakes might the children's teachers and administrators make based on the outside evaluation report?

What practices might the community mental health clinic administration want to change in order to ensure appropriate future evaluation of LEP referrals?

This case highlights several serious errors that were made in diagnosing school-related problems of LEP children.

A fundamental question must be raised about the apparent failure to interview the parents and gain their cooperation. The investigators would seemingly have been better served by first assembling the relevant details about the kinds of behavior problems displayed by the children at home and at school and then deciding on the use of appropriate assessment devices if such instruments were judged necessary. Commercially available behavior problem inventories and assessments of social skills might provide some useful information about the nature of the children's behavior problems, although there is a dearth of research in relating to Hispanic cultures. A more thorough understanding of the children's oral and written language comprehension together with their maladaptive behaviors within and outside of school would provide a much sounder basis for deciding on the proper course of treatment.

The two physicians conducting the assessment at the mental health clinic had neither the training nor the relevant experience necessary to diagnose and treat a case such as this. Neither physician understood the Spanish language or culture from which these children came. To make matters worse, a neighbor of the children, not a trained bilingual examiner, translated the test items and responses, and this in turn sacrificed strict control of the material. In addition, the neighbor's facility with English and Spanish was not clearly established prior to the testing session.

Of more basic importance is the fact that the routine use of a translator with all of the tests is questionable. For example, a translator should not have been used with the PPVT-R because this test is presumably administered to LEP children to obtain an estimate of their English receptive vocabulary. It would have been advisable for the physicians to have had the Spanish edition of the PPVT-R administered in order to obtain an estimate of their Spanish receptive vocabulary. A comparison of the English and Spanish results would have resulted in much more useful information about the children's receptive vocabulary status in both languages as well as providing some preliminary information about language dominance. Based on these preliminary results, more comprehensive measures of language facility could be administered if needed. It is also doubtful that any useful information about reading skill in English was obtained from the SORT, especially since the SORT measures only word recognition, and the test words unfamiliar to the children were translated into Spanish. Measures of reading ability in both English and Spanish, unassisted, would provide additional useful information about facility in the children's native language contrasted with their ability to comprehend written English.

More than good intentions is required to provide professionally sound assessment of LEP children. As observed with these two children, lack of adequate training in evaluating LEP children resulted in questionable conclusions based on an inappropriate selection and administration of test instruments. Such misuse of tests can only result in misdiagnosis, which in turn will most likely lead to additional inappropriate actions by school personnel. For example, placement in a special education class with insufficient reason may be the end result of a series of incorrect conclusions and actions by various well-meaning but professionally untrained and inexperienced personnel.

FACTORS INVOLVED

1. Comprehensive Assessment
2. Proper Test Use
3. Psychometric Knowledge
4. Maintaining Integrity of Test Results

ELEMENTS INVOLVED

67. Selecting tests appropriate to both the purpose of measurement and to the test takers.
47. Avoiding interpretation beyond the limits of the test.
78. Referring to a test as a basis for an interpretation only when the test has been properly administered and scored and the interpretation is well validated.
45. Choosing tests sufficient to sample behaviors for a specific purpose.
22. Knowledge of the need for multiple sources of convergent data.
23. Skill in taking a good history to integrate with test results.
5. Knowledge of legal standards.

17. Knowledge of the test and its limitations.

27. Appreciating the implications of test validity.

25. Understanding norms and their limitations.

53. Understanding the meaning of test scores in the pattern of evaluation.

68. Selecting tests that are as free from discrimination as possible, considering the standardization sample and the test-taker population.

54. Based on valid information, taking account of those elements in a test that discriminate against certain populations.

13. Refraining from modifying prescribed administration procedures to adapt to particular individuals.

5 Neuropsychological Assessment: Assessing Comprehensive Adaptive Functioning

Setting and Applications

Neuropsychology

Incident

A psychologist performed an assessment using the Wechsler Adult Intelligence Scale–Revised (WAIS-R), Bender Visual–Motor Gestalt Test, and the Rorschach. On the basis of these data, he rendered what he termed a "neuropsychological report" that included inferences regarding "normal brain functioning" in an individual who had suffered a medically verified left anterior cerebrovascular accident (i.e., stroke). Subsequently, a neuropsychological evaluation using the comprehensive Halstead-Reitan Neuropsychological Battery administered by a neuropsychologist revealed behavioral deficits clearly attributable to the patient's brain injury.

Focus Questions

What steps can those who use tests take to ensure that they are not drawn into areas of practice that are beyond their skills?

Is it conceivable that a skilled practitioner could draw appropriate inferences from an inadequate test battery? Under what circumstances might this be possible?

Neuropsychological batteries are designed to evaluate human functioning based upon behaviors that are related to different portions of the brain. The "neuropsychological test battery" employed by the psychologist in this case did not sample all those brain–behavior relationships. Indeed, a competent neuropsychologist would have predicted that the test battery used in this case was highly unlikely to reveal behavioral deficits typically caused by damage to the anterior portion of the brain. The psychologist and the patient are lucky that a competent comprehensive assessment was subsequently performed by a competent neuropsychologist. Had his condition remained improperly assessed, the patient would likely have, at the least, experienced inexplicable frustration when he proved unable to do things he was able to do prior to his illness. At worst, poor planning ability might have caused him to pose a danger to himself or others.

FACTORS INVOLVED

1. Comprehensive Assessment
2. Proper Test Use

ELEMENTS INVOLVED

22. Knowledge of the need for multiple sources of convergent data.
29. Applying principles of test theory and principles of test interpretation.
40. Refraining from making evaluations from inappropriate tests.
45. Choosing tests sufficient to sample behaviors for a specific purpose.
1. Accepting responsibility for competent use of the test.
2. Knowledge of professional ethics.
17. Knowledge of the test and its limitations.

Section 2

Training: Professional Responsibility

6 INCUMBENT TESTING FOR APPRENTICESHIP POSITIONS

SETTING AND APPLICATIONS

Employment

INCIDENT

A large organization required current employees who wanted to apply for apprenticeship positions in its machine shop to pass a mechanical comprehension test. A secretary in the personnel office loosely supervised the test program. Applicants were given the test and answer sheet, seated in the hallway, and instructed to return both to the secretary when they finished. No time limits were imposed, although the test norms were based on timed administration. Applicants sometimes complained about the legibility of the test materials, which were photocopies of originals that had been purchased several years earlier. When this happened, the secretary asked a supervisor to review the question and key and to restate the question to the applicant in the supervisor's own language. After the tests were scored, answer sheets of failing applicants were thrown in a waste basket. Answer sheets of passing applicants were placed in a folder to be used when the next apprentice class was to be filled.

The test materials were kept in an unlocked file. One supervisor used the test questions to teach mechanical principles to the supervisor's helpers. The test was also available to employees who wished to review the questions with relatives thinking of applying for the apprenticeship program.

FOCUS QUESTIONS

What kinds of policies should companies consider in order to maintain the integrity of testing programs?

What additional factors might a user consider when tests are used to evaluate incumbents?

The person in charge of industrial test programs must ensure that each examiner, each scorer, and each user of test results understands principles of good testing as they apply to each function. Unfortunately, that is not always the rule in industrial testing programs. The deceptive simplicity of paper-and-pencil testing, in particular, often leads to practices that would not be tolerated in other contexts.

Although company management believed the test requirement represented a useful standard for entrance to the apprenticeship program, lax administration made the results worthless. Whenever tests are used, a properly informed person should be in charge of administration, scoring, and all details related to the application of results. That person must be given authority to resist inappropriate pressure and must have adequate resources to maintain the integrity of the program.

The use of tests as training material generally invalidates their use for evaluation purposes. The choice of tests to be used in employee selection and promotion decisions should be guided by an understanding of the knowledges, skills, abilities, and other characteristics required by the job. Properly coordinated training and testing programs cover the same domains or content areas, but usually not identical content.

The case illustrates many other unacceptable or marginal practices. For example, although timing is tedious, it is essential that test administration maintain conditions comparable to those under which the norms were obtained. Otherwise, those norms and the test results are useless. If a test requires timed administration, the timing should be precise, not approximate. A precise timing device should be available, particularly when test administration must be completed within a few minutes. Because test security was so poor (e.g., unlocked test files, test papers discarded in waste baskets, familiarity of some employees with the test in advance), test results are likely to be completely untrustworthy.

It is a violation of federal law to photocopy test materials without the permission of the copyright holder. In addition, photocopies often put the examinee at a disadvantage. As in this case, photocopied test booklets may be illegible. Photocopied answer sheets may not fit the scoring key and may result in the examinee's receiving a wrong score.

The testing setting should be comfortable and quiet so that examinees can do their best without interruption. If examinees do not understand certain items, the test administrator should follow the directions in the test manual. Some tests allow explanations; others don't. The use of photocopied materials, apart from being illegal, is an exercise in false economy.

Finally, in today's climate, all personnel actions involve legal ramifications. In order to minimize the possibility of lawsuits, the testing program should be run according to the best interpretation of good testing practices. Records should be maintained in good order. The premature destruction of test records may make it impossible to show, for example, that the testing program was fair and nondiscriminatory.

2. Proper Test Use

1. Accepting responsibility for competent use of the test.
2. Knowledge of professional ethics.
3. Maintaining proper actions regardless of management pressures.
4. Not making photocopies of copyrighted materials.
5. Knowledge of legal standards.
6. Refraining from coaching or training individuals or groups on test items, which results in misrepresentation of the person's abilities and competencies.
8. Providing appropriate training and quality control over operations for all users of tests and test results.
12. Keeping scoring keys and test materials secure.
13. Refraining from modifying prescribed administration procedures to adapt to particular individuals.
16. Using settings for testing that allow for optimum performance by the test takers.
62. Refraining from using home-made answer sheets.
63. Following timing instructions accurately, especially for short speeded tests.

7 ASSESSING NUCLEAR POWER OPERATORS

SETTING AND APPLICATIONS

Mental Health

INCIDENT

A personnel psychologist who lacked training in the interpretation of the Minnesota Multiphasic Personality Inventory (MMPI) hired a clinical psychologist to purchase MMPI materials from the test publisher. The clinical psychologist was trained to read and interpret the test records of job applicants for nuclear power plant positions and to determine their emotional fitness for work in one of two power companies. Because of financial pressures, the personnel psychologist discontinued the use of the services of the clinical psychologist. The personnel psychologist continued to purchase the MMPI from the test publisher and did not inform the publisher that the services of the clinical psychologist had been discontinued. The test publisher's agreement to provide the test material was based on the understanding that there was ongoing consultation by the clinical psychologist, who was trained in the interpretation of the MMPI. The personnel psychologist also continued to provide the psychological screening service to the two power companies without informing those two organizations of his lack of knowledge of MMPI procedures.

FOCUS QUESTIONS

How might the personnel psychologist obtain necessary training on the MMPI?

Does the clinical psychologist have any responsibility to inform the publisher that his services are no longer being used?

Does the test publisher have any responsibility to monitor whether qualified professionals continue to be employed at sites where they have sold tests?

To prevent misuse, the personnel psychologist should have, first of all, recognized his lack of competence in the interpretation of the MMPI. This in turn should have led to several other actions. The personnel psychologist should have ceased providing MMPI-based screening services for the power companies unless and until he obtained appropriate training in MMPI interpretation. Finally, he should have ceased purchasing MMPI materials (something he was doing under false pretenses) until he received appropriate training in MMPI interpretation.

2. Proper Test Use

1. Accepting responsibility for competent use of the test.
2. Knowledge of professional ethics.
3. Maintaining proper actions regardless of management pressures.
8. Providing appropriate training and quality control over operations for all users of tests and test results.
15. Restricting test administration to qualified personnel.
17. Knowledge of the test and its limitations.

8 PRACTICING WITHIN AREAS OF COMPETENCE

Mental Health

INCIDENT
An insurance company contested the payment of claims payable to a client for extensive psychological examination and therapy. The attorney for the company charged that the psychologist involved, who had purchased and used personality assessment tests, had falsely represented herself as a clinical psychologist trained in personality assessment. She was licensed to practice in the state because she had a master's degree in experimental psychology. However, she had obtained clinical training and a PhD from a nonaccredited university. Furthermore, her academic records showed no evidence of courses, training, or supervised experience in personality assessment. Nor could the psychologist document postdoctoral training or supervision in personality assessment.

FOCUS QUESTIONS
What might the test publisher have done to identify this test purchaser who, in spite of being a licensed professional, was not competent to use the products she purchased?
How can the public be protected from individuals who practice outside their areas of competence?

Without proper training, test users may reach unsupportable conclusions and incorrect diagnoses. They may also duplicate services for which the client or third-party payer may become unnecessarily financially liable.

Regardless of practice options that may appear legally supportable (i.e., by virtue of licensing or certification), responsible professionals do not operate outside their areas of expertise. Those who wish to become familiar with assessment instruments or practices in which they were not originally trained should seek appropriate training. For example, many professional associations, universities, and other organizations offer approved continuing education programs for professionals.

FACTOR INVOLVED

2. Proper Test Use

ELEMENTS INVOLVED

1. Accepting responsibility for competent use of the test.
2. Knowledge of professional ethics.

9 THE MISDIRECTED PARENTS

SETTING AND
APPLICATIONS   Education

INCIDENT   In School District A, a large number of children are referred by their teachers for possible placement in the special educational program for educable mentally retarded (EMR) children. Guidelines indicate that children must exhibit deficits in intellectual functioning, school achievement, and adaptive behavior before they can be classified as eligible for the EMR program. School district personnel use a variety of standardized instruments, observations of behavior, assessment of school performance, and other evaluation procedures to gather comprehensive information about intelligence, achievement, and adaptive behavior.

The Vineland Adaptive Behavior Scales Survey Form, a nationally standardized, norm-referenced instrument, is used in the school district as one component of adaptive behavior assessment. The Vineland Survey Form is a rating scale administered to children's parents through a semistructured interview. During the interview, examiners ask parents to describe their children's typical activities in the domains of communication, daily living skills, socialization, and motor skills.

A professor of special education from a local college contacted parent groups in the school community and presented to them a series of workshops. During the workshops, the professor described the school district's procedures for determining EMR eligibility, including the school district's use of the Vineland Survey Form. The professor emphasized to parents that their children could not be found eligible for EMR programs, if during the Vineland interview, the parents gave responses that earned high scores for their children. The professor then gave Vineland record forms to parents, reviewed the items on the record form, and gave to the parents examples of responses that would earn high scores on the items. The professor emphasized to the parents the importance of inflating scores on the Vineland in order to prevent their children from being placed in an EMR program.

FOCUS
QUESTIONS   How did the professor's actions invalidate the Vineland results?
What actions might be taken by school district personnel to assure more accurate results from the parents that attended the professor's workshops?
Could the school district have prevented the professor from tainting the Vineland results? Are there ways to prevent this from happening in the future?
Was the professor's behavior ethical? Professional? Legal?
Could the publisher of the Vineland have prevented the professor from misusing the instrument?

Valid use of rating or interview scales, such as the Vineland, administered to parents or other third party respondents depends on respondents' providing descriptions of children's behavior that are as accurate as possible. If respondents *systematically* provide inaccurate descriptions of children's behavior, data from the scale are rendered virtually useless. Such may have been the case for parents who were administered the Vineland after participating in the professor's workshops. If parents provided inaccurate data for their children on the Vineland, a true picture of the children's adaptive behavior may not have been obtained by school district personnel. Thus, valid professional decisions about the children's needs for special services may have been affected, and the development of optimal educational programs for the children could have been jeopardized.

The professor in the incident was using the Vineland in an inappropriate manner by providing parents with Vineland record forms and helping parents earn high scores for their children, as described here:

1. The professor was inappropriately using the Vineland as a training tool to misrepresent children's competencies.

2. The professor's activities represented violations of professional standards for maintaining test security and using assessment instruments for their intended purposes.

3. By encouraging the parents to compromise the results of the assessment, the professor was encouraging misrepresentation by the parents and, possibly, was interfering with the children's rights to an appropriate evaluation with provision for needed educational services.

4. The professor was setting a poor example of his or her profession to the parents.

5. The professor's activities may also affect the parents' respect for and relationships with school personnel who use assessment instruments.

The professor's reasons for conducting the workshops and encouraging parents to invalidate the results of the Vineland are unknown. Perhaps the professor was concerned about the large number of children being referred for possible placement in the EMR program and the possible negative effect an "EMR" label can have on children. Many educators, psychologists, parents, and others share these concerns. However, there are other ways that the professor could work with parents and school professionals to address concerns about EMR classifications. Because children are typically referred for possible placement in EMR programs due to learning problems in schools, the professor could, for example, conduct workshops on techniques for preventing learning problems and could assist parents and school personnel with the development of programs that provide instructional strategies in the regular classroom for children with learning problems, without requiring that children first be classified in a special education category. If the professor believed that the school district's practices for determining eligibility for the EMR program are inappropriate, the professor could offer to assist parents and school personnel in evaluating the practices. Instead of sabotaging an assessment instrument, the professor could engage in numerous activities that promote effective educational practices for these children.

FACTOR
INVOLVED

2. Proper Test Use

ELEMENTS
INVOLVED

2. Knowledge of professional ethics.
6. Refraining from coaching or training individuals or groups on test items, which results in misrepresentation of the person's abilities and competencies.
11. Preventing individuals from reviewing actual tests prior to administration.

10 THE UNTRAINED INTERPRETER

Counseling/Training

A psychologist received a call from a career counselor at a local university counseling center. The counselor had a question about how to interpret the Infrequent Response Index on the Strong Interest Inventory. Upon further discussion, the psychologist discovered that the question about the meaning of the index had originated with the counselor's client, and because the counselor did not think that the scale was important, he had never discussed it with any client unless asked. The psychologist was surprised at the counselor's question because she knew that the counselor had been using the Strong for a number of years to help clients with career concerns and because a description of the Infrequent Response Index and how to interpret it was clearly described in both the Strong Manual and in the User's Guide.

In answer to the counselor's question about the meaning of the scale, the psychologist referred to the relevant sections of the Manual and User's Guide, whereupon she learned that the counselor did not possess copies of either document and in fact had never read either one. Further questioning revealed that his source of information about the instrument and how to interpret it derived from a survey course in vocational testing that he had successfully completed during his graduate program 4 years earlier. He had since received no training on the use of this specific instrument.

How may a counselor who is generally competent in testing acquire knowledge and skills needed to competently interpret a specific test?

What is the responsibility of publishers to determine user qualifications?

What is the responsibility of university training programs to prepare students to use tests properly?

What information from the Strong Manual or User's Guide or from a professional training program would have helped the counselor interpret the client's results?

Although the counselor may have been well-meaning in that he was truly motivated by a desire to help his clients with their career concerns, and he believed that measures of interests could be useful in this endeavor, his lack of knowledge of the instrument that he was using raised the real possibility that his interventions could do more harm than good.

Without proper preparation, the counselor may misinterpret the test results or fail to recognize the limitations of the test. With interest tests in particular, there is a danger that the client could leave the session believing that he or she should or should not enter a certain occupation or class of occupations and thus unnecessarily close off his or her options. Alternatively, the client may be led to confuse interests with abilities and believe that the scores of the interest test indicate that he or she is not qualified to perform certain tasks. As the psychologist commented when reporting this incident, "Bad information is as bad, or worse, than no information."

Acceptance of responsibility for competent use of a test means that, as a minimum, the counselor must have knowledge of the purpose of the test, how it was developed, the applicability of the test for the particular client in the particular setting in which it is to be used, the validity of the scores for the specific purpose for which they are to be employed in a given situation, as well as the specific procedures recommended for administering and interpreting the instrument. This kind of information, and more, can usually be found in the manual for the test, or in related publications that describe its use. It is the responsibility of the test user to read the test manual and other material thoroughly before using the test and then either to use the test under the supervision of a qualified practitioner until the counselor and the supervisor agree that the counselor is competent to use it, or to seek training in the use of the test. Training for specific tests is often made available by a professional organization, the test publisher, or an independent training organization.

Because the reasons for the counselor's behavior are not evident from the facts of this case, it is not possible to assign a specific motive to his behavior, and therefore not possible to say exactly what could have prevented the test misuse. Perhaps he received the impression in his testing course that he was competent to use the Strong after a brief survey. Or perhaps he was simply not motivated to take the time to improve his knowledge of the test, having underestimated the potential harm that could accrue from misinformation about interests. Another possibility is that he may have been unaware that in addition to violating standards of proper test use, he was in danger of transgressing an ethical principle. Performing only services for which one is competent is an ethical principle of many professional organizations.

2. Proper Test Use

17. Knowledge of the test and its limitations.
1. Accepting responsibility for competent use of the test.
2. Knowledge of professional ethics.

11 Use of Computer-Based Test Interpretations

Setting and Applications

Employment

Incident

A business organization decided to use clinical assessment to evaluate employees for jobs involving considerable stress and requiring teamwork, dependability, and good judgment. The organization's test specialist decided to use the Minnesota Multiphasic Personality Inventory (MMPI) and a computerized MMPI scoring service for this purpose. He then hired a qualified clinician to aid in evaluating the MMPI results.

The clinician used the MMPI as the initial screening procedure. She considered demographic moderators in her interpretation of the profile, especially when norms were inconsistent with the educational level of individual applicants. She also considered the applicant's work history and conducted interviews where necessary. The computer service corrected MMPI scores for certain stylistic or response tendencies and employed norms collected by the author of the interpretation program. When she compared that profile with the uncorrected profile, there were major discrepancies in the resulting interpretations. The introduction to the computerized narrative advised users not to base decisions solely on the report. Nevertheless, the clinician judged that some statements were presented in an unqualified manner.

When the clinician attempted to determine the basis for the computer-generated narrative, she was unable to do so. The scoring service did not routinely provide algorithms or configural rules for the interpretations. From material supplied by the service, she was able to find general references on the scales. However, the clinician concluded that validity evidence for several scales used in the computer report was not well documented in the manual or supplementary materials provided by the service.

Focus Questions

What should the clinician recommend to the client organization?

What kind of information should computer interpretation services routinely provide to their clients?

What approach might be taken by the clinician and client organization to evaluate the computerized interpretations of job applicants?

The clinician in this case was conscientious in her attempts to establish the validity of the computer report and was justified in her caution. Test users in industry need to meet the objectives of their employer while maintaining the high standards of their profession. They should consult the *Standards for Educational and Psychological Testing* (*Standards*, 1985) for guidance. Standard 5.11 states that "Organizations offering automated test interpretation should make available information on the rationale of the test and a summary of the evidence supporting the interpretations given." The publisher of the computer-based test interpretation system and the author of this system bear the professional responsibility for meeting this standard. However, test users must inevitably decide when the standard has been met.

Test users must ask themselves: What evidence for the validity of this report exists? Is this the kind of product that is useful for the purpose I have in mind? What hypotheses should be followed up in an interview? Do some narrative statements not apply to this person? Are the norms appropriate? What further information do I need? Are some narrative statements overstated?

Test users must consider both the strengths and the limitations of interpretative test services and the appropriateness of reports for each application. Before deciding to use a service or specific report, they should review published material provided by the service. If the published material is incomplete, they should request additional information from the service and discuss their concerns with the service's professional staff. They might also evaluate the appropriateness of computerized interpretations on a sample of persons with well-documented case histories prior to approving them for routine use. Unless they are convinced that the evidence supporting the interpretations is satisfactory, they should avoid using the service or report.

In addition to concerns about the computerized report, this case raises broader questions about the scope of assessment. The evaluation involved several different criteria (i.e., stress coping ability, teamwork, dependability, and good judgment). Despite a decision made by the organization's testing specialist, a single instrument or method may not be able to assess all criteria adequately. In this case, the clinician used an interview to supplement the MMPI. Additional measures (e.g., cognitive ability tests, normal-range personality scales) could provide a firmer basis for reaching conclusions about the applicant's judgment or teamwork skills. The test user needs to consider these factors carefully in the design of an assessment system.

FACTORS INVOLVED

6. Appropriate Use of Norms
1. Comprehensive Assessment
3. Psychometric Knowledge

ELEMENTS INVOLVED

70. Detecting and rejecting errors and overstatements in English narratives produced by computer software.
84. Integrating the computer printout with other results, rather than presenting the printout as a report.
83. Being concerned with the individual differences of test takers, rather than presenting test scores directly from descriptions in the manual or computer printout.
27. Appreciating the implications of test validity.
25. Understanding norms and their limitations.

12 THE STAR-STRUCK CLINICIAN

SETTING AND APPLICATIONS Mental Health

INCIDENT A mental health clinician with expertise in projective testing was asked to appear on a television show dealing with the mental health problems of adolescents. Among other things, he was asked to demonstrate the administration of the Rorschach Inkblot Test to a disturbed adolescent. The situation was portrayed as a spontaneous administration of the test: Each card was shown for about 5 seconds on the screen and then superimposed on the subject's face as she responded. The mental health clinician was identified by his real name; the subject was played by a professional actress and given a fictitious name.

FOCUS QUESTIONS What are the implications of this case for appropriately educating the public about personality testing?

How might showing the Rorschach cards on television affect the validity of the test for other individuals?

What steps might the psychologist have taken to protect the security of the Rorschach cards before, during, and after his TV appearance?

The value of psychological tests and other assessment devices depends in part on the unfamiliarity of the subject with the tests. Thus, testing professionals should make every effort to maintain the security of tests. The broadcast of the Rorschach cards potentially compromised the validity of the technique for a significant sector of the population.

The mental health clinician had been told that there would be brief close-up shots of the test situation, but did not learn until after the telecast that the actual Rorschach cards had been shown. The mental health practitioner should have determined exactly how the test was to be used and, at the least, counseled the producers of the television show not to misuse the test materials. A better solution would have been to use a set of inkblots created for the demonstration.

2. Proper Test Use

11. Preventing individuals from reviewing actual tests prior to administration.
12. Keeping scoring keys and test materials secure.
2. Knowledge of professional ethics.

13 DEALING WITH THE PRESS

SETTING AND
APPLICATIONS
Mental Health

INCIDENT
An expert gave information about a figure drawing test to a freelance writer, who was writing an article. The psychologist was under the impression that the article would be a dignified, general statement about how such tests help mental health professionals provide services to the public. Instead, the article appeared in a magazine under a banner heading: "Figure Out Your Own Personality." It provided blank space for drawings, gave instructions about scoring, and showed illustrative drawings.

FOCUS
QUESTIONS
What could the testing expert do to prevent similar outcomes when working with other members of the media?
Members of the media, who operate under tight deadlines, often do not provide interviewees with the opportunity to preview articles. In view of that, is there anything the testing expert could have done to assure accuracy of the information prior to its publication?

Although the test expert did not intend to violate any principle of good testing practice, he underestimated the dangers inherent in popularizing projective techniques. More specifically, he failed to preview the article prior to its publication, at which time he could have talked to the author about inappropriate use of the material.

It is always wise when talking to laypersons to be especially careful about what information one conveys about tests. It is easy for experts waxing eloquent about their favorite topic to lose sight of the fact that they will probably be most helpful and informative if they convey a modicum of information in language that is as simple as possible. Professionals who are unused to dealing with the media on such matters would be well advised to seek the counsel of a more experienced colleague.

Testing professionals should make sure that tests and test results are used only by those capable of using them properly. This does not mean restricting the use of tests to persons with specified credentials. It does mean that one must carefully specify the knowledges, skills, abilities, and other characteristics required to use a given test properly and be equally careful in making sure that proposed users possess those characteristics. Obviously, this means restricting self-application of personality tests by inexperienced magazine readers.

FACTOR INVOLVED

2. Proper Test Use

ELEMENTS INVOLVED

8. Providing appropriate training and quality control over operations for all users of tests and test results.
15. Restricting test administration to qualified personnel.
2. Knowledge of professional ethics.

14 POOR VOCABULARY NEEDS ATTENTION

SETTING AND APPLICATIONS

Speech-Language-Hearing

INCIDENT

A speech-language pathologist with 5 years of clinical experience, working in a public school setting, was hired by a community to test children as part of a preventive preschool program instituted by the community special education coordinator. The community was, for example, predominantly White in its racial composition, although there were some minority residents.

The clinician administered the Peabody Picture Vocabulary Test–Revised (PPVT-R), a test that measures single word receptive vocabulary, to an American Indian preschool child. When the clinician scored the test, she found that, based on the PPVT-R norms, the child scored one standard deviation below the average for his age group. The case history revealed a previous mild middle ear infection, with no apparent effect on communication development. There was no reported history of communication disorders in the child's family. The clinician reported the PPVT-R score to the special education coordinator and the parents, with the recommendation that the child receive speech-language services to remediate his difficulty.

FOCUS QUESTIONS

How might a child's American Indian background affect the way the child performed on the PPVT-R?

How might the speech-language pathologist have confirmed her diagnosis and supported her recommendations that the child receive speech-language services?

The child's cultural background was taken into account neither during the test selection process, the test situation itself, nor the test result interpretation process. Because the PPVT-R is not standardized on an American Indian population, an alternative test with such norms is another possible, although not completely satisfactory, solution. The use of observations and interviews with the child's significant others as well as comparing the child with other children in the community with similar backgrounds and experiences is an important aspect of the evaluation process to include in such cases.

Although the child's behavior during the test was not mentioned by the tester, experience in test taking and motivation to play the test game are important factors to consider when administering standardized tests to persons from a nondominant culture.

The problem was compounded by using the inappropriate norms to decide the child had a communication disorder that required remediation services. Such a decision should not have been made on the basis of a single test, especially one that was not designed as a diagnostic test for language disorders. In reporting the test score to the special education coordinator and the parents, the speech-language pathologist failed to indicate that the results might not truly reflect the child's vocabulary level because the norms of the test were derived from a population with a different cultural background from the child's. The clinician could have indicated that the test results told more about what the child knew about "mainstream" vocabulary.

The speech-language pathologist should have considered the results of several tests and case history information before making a diagnosis of a communication disorder, with the accompanying recommendation for treatment. The PPVT-R assesses only single word receptive vocabulary and not a broad range of speech and language skills.

FACTORS INVOLVED

1. Comprehensive Assessment
2. Proper Test Use
3. Psychometric Knowledge
6. Appropriate Use of Norms
7. Interpretive Feedback

ELEMENTS INVOLVED

40. Refraining from making evaluations from inappropriate tests.
45. Choosing tests sufficient to sample behaviors for a specific purpose.
86. Refraining from reporting scores to administrators without adequate interpretation.
17. Knowledge of the test and its limitations.
25. Understanding norms and their limitations.
68. Selecting tests that are as free from discrimination as possible, considering the standardization sample and the test-taker population.
67. Selecting tests appropriate to both the purpose of measurement and to the test takers.
46. Interpreting test results properly for the particular group tested, keeping in mind the characteristics of that group.

15 THE ERRANT INSTRUCTOR

SETTING AND APPLICATIONS

Mental Health

INCIDENT

A graduate student in a field that uses projective tests reported to the central ethics committee for her profession that she had observed undergraduate students administering and interpreting the Rorschach Inkblot Test to other students in the dormitory where she was a resident advisor. She indicated that she had learned from one student that their instructor for an undergraduate course in the psychology of individual differences had given them the Rorschach cards.

FOCUS QUESTIONS

What might the central ethics committee do to see that the instructor does not make the same mistake again?
Are there circumstances under which the instructor's actions might be acceptable?

The instructor who provided the Rorschach cards to his students later said that he could see nothing wrong with what he was doing. This seems contrary to the written policies regarding testing promulgated by virtually all professional bodies whose members use tests. His actions suggest that he was ignorant of professional standards regarding test use or else was an incompetent professional.

The instructor in this case was inadvertently promoting the use of psychological assessment techniques by insufficiently trained persons. The undertrained are at risk for making inappropriate interpretations—which may lead to inappropriate decisions—of all kinds based on misunderstanding of the test results. This danger is compounded when the test deals with unfamiliar concepts.

Testing professionals should make sure that tests and test results are used only by those capable of using them properly. This does not mean restricting the use of tests to persons with specified credentials. It does mean that one must carefully specify the knowledges, skills, abilities, and other characteristics required to use a given test properly and be equally careful in making sure that proposed users possess those characteristics.

FACTOR INVOLVED

2. Proper Test Use

ELEMENTS INVOLVED

1. Accepting responsibility for competent use of the test.
2. Knowledge of professional ethics.
8. Providing appropriate training and quality control over operations for all users of tests and test results.
15. Restricting test administration to qualified personnel.
17. Knowledge of the test and its limitations.
12. Keeping scoring keys and test materials secure.

16 THE MYSTERY OF THE MISSING DATA

SETTING AND APPLICATIONS

Neuropsychology

INCIDENT

A mental health professional employed by a private clinic for emotionally disturbed children developed a test to assess certain aspects of brain damage. The test was similar to several other well-established instruments designed to measure brain damage, although not so similar as to constitute an infringement of copyright. The mental health professional did not perform any studies to substantiate his test's validity. He set up a computer program to score and interpret the instrument. In marketing the program, he attached a disclaimer to the package to the effect that "validation efforts are continuing."

Another mental health professional purchased the test and noticed the disclaimer as she began to try out the test for the first time. She complained that the test should not be offered for sale until there was some research substantiating its validity.

FOCUS QUESTIONS

What might the test author do to show the validity of his instrument for the purpose for which he proposes it be used?

With what bodies might the test user lodge a formal complaint about the marketing of the test?

In response to the complaint, the test author explained that he had attached the disclaimer to the computer program precisely to avoid this problem. He wished to be sure his colleagues purchasing the program knew that the test was still in an experimental stage and that validation studies remained to be done. He did not wish to deceive anyone and regretted that the complainant had not noticed the disclaimer before she purchased the test. He could not respond satisfactorily when asked why he had worded the disclaimer so that it implied that some validation studies had been performed, an unethical practice at best.

The potential for harm of putting unvalidated tests into the hands of clinicians making important decisions about clients should be self-evident. The assessment of brain damage, in particular, may be a life-or-death matter. One cannot rely on similarity (of items) to validated tests to substantiate prescriptive or prognostic use of a new test. Truth in advertising is incumbent on test authors and test publishers no less than on anyone else trying to sell a product. Experimental tests, in particular, must be unmistakably labeled as such. Also, test purchasers need to read all documentation carefully before using a test.

1. Comprehensive Assessment
2. Proper Test Use
3. Psychometric Knowledge
4. Maintaining Integrity of Test Results
6. Appropriate Use of Norms

47. Avoiding interpretation beyond the limits of the test.
78. Referring to a test as a basis for an interpretation only when the test has been properly administered and scored and the interpretation is well validated.
1. Accepting responsibility for competent use of the test.
14. Evaluating tests and detecting misleading promotional material.
27. Appreciating the implications of test validity.
48. Refraining from using a research version of a test without norms for a non-English-speaking group to make placement decisions for such a group.
69. Detecting and rejecting unvalidated norms in an unauthorized computer scoring program for a standardized test that is marketed with novel, "home-grown" norms to avoid copyright liability.

17 THE UNINFORMED INSTRUCTORS

SETTING AND APPLICATIONS   Neuropsychology

INCIDENT   At an invited seminar, an expert in testing for brain damage suggested that the cognitive retraining specialists use the Wisconsin Card Sort to identify problems in high-level cognitive processing. They also used the Wisconsin Card Sort as an outcome measure to gauge the efficiency of their training efforts. The retraining specialists recognized the need to evaluate, and attempt to rehabilitate, such cognitive processes. Knowing of no other tools to use, they pressed the Wisconsin Card Sort into service as rehabilitation tool, teaching brain-damaged individuals how to complete the test accurately.

FOCUS QUESTIONS   Why does teaching brain-damaged individuals how to complete the test accurately diminish the test's utility as a diagnostic or evaluation device?

How could the retraining specialists have identified other assessment tools that tap the same function as the Wisconsin Card Sort?

The value of tests and other assessment devices depends in part on the unfamiliarity of the subject with the tests. Using the Wisconsin Card Sort as a cognitive retraining tool destroys its value as an assessment technique for the clients in question. In this case, the cognitive retraining specialists themselves were aware of no other tools for assessing high-level cognitive functions, making it impossible for them to evaluate the efficacy of their rehabilitation efforts. Rather than compromising the only assessment tool they had, the retraining specialists should have sought materials designed specifically for retraining functions like those assessed by the Wisconsin Card Sort. Although tests should rarely, if ever, be used as therapeutic tools, the retraining specialists should have looked for another assessment tool that taps the same functions as the Wisconsin Card Sort if they believed that no appropriate training materials were available or could be easily devised.

FACTOR INVOLVED

2. Proper Test Use

ELEMENTS INVOLVED

6. Refraining from coaching or training individuals or groups on test items, which results in misrepresentation of the person's abilities and competencies.
11. Preventing individuals from reviewing actual tests prior to administration.

18 ASSESSING THE WRONG "PROBLEM"

SETTING AND APPLICATIONS

Neuropsychology

INCIDENT

An individual working in a private mental health practice administered a battery of tests to assess a post-acute brain-injured client for learning problems. Subsequently, a specialist in the assessment of brain damage was called to testify on behalf of the plaintiff (the brain-injured client) in a personal injury lawsuit. As part of his assessment, the specialist reviewed the report written by the original examiner. The specialist concluded that the original examiner had a poor understanding of brain–behavior relationships and the use of psychometric tests in the assessment of brain damage. The specialist indicated that the examiner had drawn conclusions about the client's potential for rehabilitation based on an insufficient and inappropriate sample of the client's capabilities. The specialist characterized the original examiner's report as reflecting gross incompetence in the assessment of brain injury.

It came to light during the trial that the original examiner, who worked subordinate to better-educated professionals in the private mental health practice, felt implied pressure to accept the assessment referral from a more senior colleague in order to "keep the fee within the practice." Characterizing the referral question as learning problems was a ruse on the part of the referring colleague to create the appearance that the original examiner was practicing within his areas of competence.

FOCUS QUESTION

What arguments might the subordinate have used with his superior in an effort to avoid becoming involved in an assessment task for which he was not fully qualified?

The assessment of brain injury is often a matter of life and death. Fortunately, that was not the case here. However, the first examiner's report could have led to an incorrect verdict in the personal injury case. It could have led also to inappropriate rehabilitation efforts, perhaps as a result of incorrect prognostic statements.

The original examiner should have indicated to his more senior colleague that he could not competently perform the desired assessment. If the colleague persisted, the examiner should have asked for help in making his case. He could have appealed for help from other local professional colleagues and if necessary could have approached the national professional association or the state licensing board for his profession.

FACTORS INVOLVED

1. Comprehensive Assessment
2. Proper Test Use
3. Psychometric Knowledge

ELEMENTS INVOLVED

30. Resisting political pressures to shorten the planning, diagnostic, and interpretive process unduly.
2. Knowledge of professional ethics.
53. Understanding the meaning of test scores in the pattern of evaluation.
46. Interpreting test results properly for the particular group tested, keeping in mind the characteristics of that group.

19 La Belle Indifference?

SETTING AND APPLICATIONS

Neuropsychology

INCIDENT

A specialist in testing for brain dysfunctions was asked to assess a patient with atypical symptoms. The neuropsychiatrist whom the patient originally consulted was initially of the opinion that the patient was suffering from a classical Conversion Disorder whose primary symptom—seizures—was functional in origin. Nevertheless, exhibiting appropriate caution, the neuropsychiatrist referred the patient for a neurological examination that included an electroencephalogram. The neurologist felt that the results of his examination were equivocal: He could not confidently rule in or rule out an organically based seizure disorder. The neurological consultant recommended referral to a specialist in testing for brain dysfunctions in order to obtain another diagnostic opinion.

The patient was referred to a mental health specialist who claimed expertise in testing for brain dysfunctions. The mental health specialist administered the Luria-Nebraska Neuropsychological Battery (LNNB). On the basis of those results, he concluded that the patient was not suffering from an organically based seizure disorder and rendered the opinion that she was, in fact, suffering from a Conversion Disorder. Conservative psychological treatment resulted in no improvement in the patient's condition. Finally, the original neuropsychiatrist and neurologist decided that a trial of antiseizure medication was warranted. The medication brought the patient's seizures rapidly under control. Reexamination of the case data by an internal quality assurance team revealed that the mental health specialist who had administered the LNNB had miscalculated one of the most important scores. Unfortunately, it was impossible to determine whether he made other errors.

FOCUS QUESTION

How might test scoring errors, like the one presented in this case, be avoided?

The mental health specialist who administered the LNNB believed that attending a 2-day workshop and reading the test manual qualified him to administer and interpret the test. (He had no other training in the assessment of brain dysfunctions.) The mental health specialist also failed to administer personality tests (e.g., MMPI, Rorschach) or conduct a clinical interview in his efforts to determine the cause of the patient's seizures.

Seizures are often life-threatening. The mental health specialist's overconfidence may have placed the patient in this case in danger of losing her life and even placed others in similar danger (e.g., if she were to have a seizure while driving) during the period before medication was prescribed.

Testing professionals must recognize their own limitations as well as the limitations of their assessment tools. The mental health specialist needed much more training in fields like neuroanatomy, brain–behavior relationships, and test-based assessment of brain injury before trying to establish the presence of brain damage without appropriate supervision.

FACTORS INVOLVED

1. Comprehensive Assessment
2. Proper Test Use
5. Accuracy of Scoring

ELEMENTS INVOLVED

22. Knowledge of the need for multiple sources of convergent data.
47. Avoiding interpretation beyond the limits of the test.
78. Referring to a test as a basis for an interpretation only when the test has been properly administered and scored and the interpretation is well validated.
17. Knowledge of the test and its limitations.
55. Avoiding errors in scoring and recording.

20 NO SIGN OF TROUBLE

SETTING AND
APPLICATIONS
Speech-Language-Hearing

INCIDENT
A school psychologist was asked to administer an individual intelligence test to an 8-year-old girl with a severe sensorineural (affecting the cochlea or neural system) hearing loss. The psychologist felt qualified to work with this child because his training had included a course related to the needs of special populations. During the testing, the child wore binaural (both ears) hearing aids, and the tester was careful to have his face clearly visible and well-lighted to allow the student to speechread adequately. At the risk of violating the standardization of the test, the examiner supplemented his instructions at times with gestures and pantomime, while articulating the directions very carefully and loudly. The tester was confident that the student understood because she nodded and smiled in agreement when he spoke to her. The student obtained test scores in the lower extreme (i.e., standard scores below 70). Because of his efforts and the fact that the testing seemed to be valid, the psychologist concluded that the girl's test scores accurately reflected her intellectual abilities and recommended placement appropriate to her level of test performance.

**FOCUS
QUESTIONS**
How could the school psychologist have confirmed that the student understood the testing directions?

Beyond one course related to the needs of special populations, what types of knowledges, skills, abilities, and other personal characteristics should the examiner have in order to adequately test students with hearing impairments?

This case demonstrates that, despite good intentions in test administration, a lack of adequate knowledge and training with a special population may lead to inappropriate testing conditions and potentially inaccurate interpretation of test results. The training of an examiner for students with hearing impairments should include graduate-level courses and supervised clinical experience with individuals with hearing impairments as well as training to become competent in the preferred mode of communication of the students, such as sign language. It is encouraging to note that the psychologist recognized the need to be certain that the test instructions were understood and the test results were valid. However, the school psychologist should have consulted an audiologist; such consultation would have afforded him information about the child's hearing abilities and how to modify the testing environment appropriately. The school psychologist assumed that, but did not know if, the hearing aids were functional and what was the preferred mode of communication of the client. He did not know if the student habitually used oral communication and speechreading or depended on some other communication mode, such as American Sign Language (ASL), signed exact English, and so on. Although the use of gestures and pantomime accompanying speech does help the comprehension of persons with hearing impairments to a limited degree, it would be of limited value to a person using ASL. Skilled sign language users score significantly higher when tests are administered using ASL. In addition, the tester did not realize that normal, relaxed speech is easier to speechread than overarticulated speech and that persons with hearing impairments have been conditioned to nod and smile in agreement even when they do not understand what is being said to them.

Assuming that the low test scores of a person with a hearing impairment reflect lower abilities is unfortunately not an uncommon mistake. Modifying the test administration, even if not appropriately modified, can lead to a false sense of confidence in the test results. Tests used with individuals with hearing impairments must be selected and administered to ensure that the test results reflect the factors the test purports to measure and that the test results do not simply reflect the hearing impairment.

It is important that examiners of students with hearing impairments have adequate training and information to administer tests and make valid interpretations of the results. Without an examiner available to administer a test in the student's preferred mode of communication, an alternative (though a less desirable one) is for the examiner to use an interpreter who is skilled both in the client's preferred mode of communication and in communicating with persons who are hearing impaired. Under these circumstances, the client can use his or her own mode of communication.

Examiners need to be cognizant of the special test needs of clients with auditory problems and should work closely with the audiologist, speech-language pathologist, teacher for the hearing impaired, parents, and other members of the student's interdisciplinary team. They should select tests that are appropriate for individuals with a hearing impairment and should use caution in making test interpretations.

FACTORS INVOLVED

1. Proper Test Use
2. Comprehensive Assessment

ELEMENTS INVOLVED

15. Restricting test administration to qualified personnel.
22. Knowledge of the need for multiple sources of convergent data.
82. Presenting or reporting "clinical" observations made during testing only if the test user supports the observations by adequate background and knowledge.

21 THE SLICK SALESMAN

SETTING AND
APPLICATIONS

Employment

INCIDENT

Sam applied for a position as a sales representative for a large company in Los Angeles. The personnel staff advised him that all candidates completed the California Psychological Inventory (CPI) as part of the application process. Sam told the staff person that he had a very important appointment and would not have time to complete the test at that time. He asked whether he could take the test with him and return it later. The staff person was not sure that this was acceptable. However, Sam was very persuasive.

Sam immediately identified the CPI publisher from the address on the answer sheet. He phoned a customer service representative who told him that the CPI was a restricted instrument. Sam requested a copy of the qualifications form, which was sent to him with a catalog. He studied the test distribution policy carefully and determined what he thought would meet the publisher's requirements for release of the materials. By lying about his training and experience on the qualification form, Sam was able to meet the publisher's criteria.

As soon as he had established his qualifications, Sam purchased a CPI manual and a set of hand-scoring keys. He studied the scale descriptions and decided what would be a good profile for a salesperson. With the help of the test keys, he completed the items accordingly. Sam then returned the answer sheet to a personnel staff person at the company, who arranged to have it scored.

The company hired Sam, who did well, and promoted him later. The facts of the case only came to light a few years later when Sam bragged to someone who had friends in the test publishing industry about how he had outsmarted the system.

FOCUS
QUESTIONS

What could the Los Angeles company have done to improve test security?
What can publishers and professionals do to ensure that test purchasers are qualified to use the test?

Sam's behavior in lying about his credentials was obviously improper. However, beyond his unprincipled behavior, this case raises important questions about what test administrators and publishers need to do in order to maintain test security.

The problem began when the personnel staff allowed Sam to take the booklet and answer sheet with him. All administration procedures should be standardized so that results are comparable across applicants. Off-site testing introduces many unacceptable risks. For example, the company had no assurance that the answers were those of the candidate. In addition, other job candidates might become aware of the content of the items. This would invalidate the company's use of the test for selection purposes and possibly compromise other testing programs that relied upon CPI results.

This case also raises the question about how far a publisher should go to protect test security. Those involved in high-stakes programs whose results are used for admission to undergraduate and graduate programs or for licensing must maintain a very high degree of security. Booklets and answer sheets are shipped only to designated testing centers and accounted for before and after testing. Test items change regularly so that all examinees are assessed fairly.

Whether or not they manage high-stakes programs, reputable test publishers have established policies designed to ensure that material is sold only to qualified individuals. Specific procedures differ across publishers. Typically, a publisher uses a form designed to elicit information about the potential customer's educational background and experience. Applicants often sign a statement that the information that they have provided is accurate. Current practices, however, do not always include extensive verification of this information. Test publishers do not usually require transcripts or other written proof from third parties that could be used to verify the statements made on the qualification forms.

It is not clear from the facts of the case to what extent the CPI results contributed to the hiring decision. Test results should only be one source of information about a potential job candidate. They must be interpreted in the context of all the information known about the individual. However, this is not always made clear to applicants. Sam's behavior illustrates a common examinee perception that the test is the primary criterion for employment. Although it is sometimes difficult to convince examinees otherwise, it is important that test users establish rapport with each one and explain that many factors will contribute to the final decision.

FACTOR INVOLVED

2. Proper Test Use

ELEMENTS INVOLVED

2. Knowledge of professional ethics.

8. Providing appropriate training and quality control over operations for all users of tests and test results.

11. Preventing individuals from reviewing actual tests prior to administration.

12. Keeping scoring keys and test materials secure.

15. Restricting test administration to qualified personnel.

78. Referring to a test as a basis for an interpretation only when the test has been properly administered and scored and the interpretation is well validated.

22 PERSONNEL SCREENING FOR EMOTIONAL STABILITY

Employment

INCIDENT

The test development branch of a state civil service agency received a request from the state correctional agency. The request was to develop a psychological screening procedure for use as part of the process of selecting correctional officers. The assessment procedure was to be used to identify people unfit for this highly stressful, emotionally demanding job. The manager assigned to this project began by reviewing the research literature on personality assessment in various employment settings (including jobs in the area of corrections) and by reading test reviews. She also discussed the proposed screening program with more than 10 other experts located throughout the United States.

The next step was to conduct a job analysis. Through this process, the project manager identified a dozen job-related personal characteristics of correctional officers. She also described potential rejection indicators and possible job difficulties. The purpose of the assessment procedure was to screen out persons who were likely to be unstable, dangerous, or violent. Finally, she selected two objective personality measures for which an extensive research history existed. In addition, evidence from background investigations and interviews were included among the screening components. An extensive manual described the entire assessment system for those actually conducting the screening.

The project manager worked directly with the personnel director who would be doing the screening. This person was very familiar with the correctional officer position and also had a background in testing. For these reasons, the personnel director was able to understand readily how to interpret the results of the testing. Before starting, the project manager and the personnel director reviewed the results of the job analysis, the testing instruments, and the nature of the other information to be used. Examiners trained in the use of the two personality measures in clinical assessment conducted the evaluations using the job analysis results.

**FOCUS
QUESTIONS**

What aspects of the screening program would be essential to document in the manual?
Of what value was the manager's review of the research literature on personality assessment in various employment settings?

This case illustrates how screening should be done. The test development project manager understood the limits of her expertise. She consulted relevant research literature and experts in the field. She worked closely with the personnel director whose knowledge of the job was extensive. She also made certain that the personnel director understood the basis for the selection decisions. In doing so, she met the needs of the organization in a very sensitive and thoughtful manner.

One activity that was not discussed but that would be quite helpful to the success of the program would be to plan follow-up data collection. This would provide additional data to support the screening program and monitor its performance across possible changes in organizational needs and applicant pools.

FACTORS INVOLVED

2. Proper Test Use
3. Psychometric Knowledge
1. Comprehensive Assessment

ELEMENTS INVOLVED

15. Restricting test administration to qualified personnel.
22. Knowledge of the need for multiple sources of convergent data.
67. Selecting tests appropriate to both the purpose of the measurement and to the test takers.

23 DISPOSITION OF PSYCHOLOGICAL TEST REPORTS

SETTING AND APPLICATIONS

Employment

INCIDENT

An expert on organizations and personnel was hired by a large company to write a report that would analyze the organizational structure of the company and the manner of interaction among various key personnel in the company. The expert wrote the report, which contained psychological profiles derived from test results of individual executives. The report existed as one original with no duplicate copies and was kept locked in the expert's desk for safekeeping. The original was subsequently given to the chief executive officer (CEO) with verbal comments about the sensitivity of some of the findings. Although the report was marked with large red letters stating that the results were confidential, no written or verbal discussion of the need for maintaining security was delivered. Two years later, the company was sold. The expert was not aware of the sale. The new CEO called the expert and expressed admiration for the quality of the report and indicated that the CEO had distributed copies to some of the top management staff of the organization. The expert found out that the former CEO had left the report on the desk for the new CEO to find and to do with as the new CEO saw fit.

FOCUS QUESTIONS

What steps could the consultant have taken to ensure the confidentiality of the original report?

What recommendations could the consultant offer the new CEO regarding the use of the report?

This case is a good example of the difficulty that consultants have in maintaining ethical standards for test use in an organization after they no longer have a direct association. The expert should have taken explicit steps to educate the former CEO and the organization about the need to respect the confidentiality of reports such as the one in this case. Consultants need to be conscious of the fact that their association with a company is often temporary. Reports need to be written with an awareness of the limited ability of the consultant to control later distribution and use of the report. Also, the employees providing the data need to know what risks are associated with such studies and that the personal risks will be minimized by the consultant's careful writing of the report. Finally, if very sensitive information is disclosed, it may not be advisable to have a written report summarizing that information. Instead, a verbal summary may need to be the only form of reporting to the CEO. If a consultant obtains information and promises security, the report must be in a form that guarantees that security.

FACTORS INVOLVED

2. Proper Test Use
4. Maintaining Integrity of Test Results

ELEMENTS INVOLVED

1. Accepting responsibility for competent use of the test.
8. Providing appropriate training and quality control over operations for all users of tests and test results.
12. Keeping scoring keys and test materials secure.

24 USE OF TESTS REQUIRES PSYCHOMETRIC KNOWLEDGE

SETTING AND APPLICATIONS

Education

INCIDENT

An assistant superintendent reported to the school board that the school district had made great strides in reading instruction during the previous year. The evidence that he used to support his claim was that the average grade equivalents obtained from the year's administration of the Stanford Achievement Test were just slightly less than one grade equivalent unit higher than the average grade equivalents from prior years. When the district's testing coordinator heard the assistant superintendent's evidence, he realized that the assistant superintendent's conclusions were most likely unwarranted for the following reasons: (a) There was a high probability that the slight increase in grade equivalents could have occurred by chance or measurement error; (b) grade equivalents, being ordinal measures, are not the best scores to measure changes in performance over time; and (c) comparisons of student performance over time are difficult to interpret because scores tend to become inflated when the same edition of a test is used over a period of years. The testing coordinator met privately with the assistant superintendent to express his concerns. The assistant superintendent listened politely and expressed regret that he had not known that the slight gain in grade equivalents might be of questionable significance.

FOCUS QUESTIONS

What are some actions that the assistant superintendent could have taken to prevent his misinterpretation of test results?

What might be some factors that cause test scores to increase as the length of time since norming increases?

What method other than grade equivalent scores could be used to support the effectiveness of instruction?

The testing coordinator's concerns about the test scores were correct, and he acted appropriately in meeting privately with the assistant superintendent to voice his concerns. It would have been even more appropriate if the testing coordinator had met with the assistant superintendent *before* he made his report to the school board, in order to prevent the presentation of misleading information to the school board. If the assistant superintendent's claims were accepted by the school board and general public as scientific evidence, an inaccurate picture of the school district's progress in reading instruction would be obtained, poor decisions about instructional programs and students might be made, and this type of misuse of test scores might be repeated. The assistant superintendent should inform the school board that the initial interpretive information provided to them was incorrect.

Because the assistant superintendent's job entails the use and interpretation of test scores, he must acquire sufficient knowledge about the technical properties of tests so that he can interpret test results properly and seek consultative assistance when necessary. Any person who uses and interprets tests scores must adhere to and promote appropriate testing practices and must refrain from inappropriate use of tests or test results for the purpose of making a system or instructional program look good.

2. Proper Test Use
3. Psychometric Knowledge
4. Maintaining Integrity of Proper Test Use

1. Accepting responsibility for competent use of the test.
3. Maintaining proper actions regardless of management pressures.
8. Providing appropriate training and quality control over operations for all users of tests and test results.
9. Resisting pressures to amass higher scores than justified to make the system "look good."
17. Knowledge of the test and its limitations.
39. Advising administrators about the limitations of norms, especially grade equivalents, for student populations differing markedly from the norm sample.
50. Interpreting differences among scores in terms of the standard error concept.
53. Understanding the meaning of test scores in the pattern of evaluation.

25 A SENSITIVE SCHOOL PSYCHOLOGIST

SETTING AND APPLICATIONS   Education

INCIDENT   Janie, an 8-year-old girl, was referred to a multidisciplinary team by her guidance counselor and teachers for evaluation of her avoidant behavior and assessment of her intellectual potential. When collecting background information about Janie, the school psychologist on the multidisciplinary team found that she refused to read aloud, cried persistently, performed erratically, and failed to follow directions in class. Her teachers indicated that she "blocked herself off" by flatly refusing to participate in class. They characterized her as strong-willed, yet extremely shy and unsure of herself. The school-based resource teacher was solicited to work with her, but Janie would not speak to the teacher. Her mother noted that Janie had been ridiculed when younger due to a speech articulation problem. Janie had been referred to a private psychologist for evaluation, but she refused to cooperate with testing and no results were obtained. The psychologist labeled her as "untestable."

The school psychologist observed and evaluated Janie over the course of several months. At the outset, she cried profusely and turned her back when the school psychologist visited the classroom. During the following few weeks, the school psychologist visited the classroom and sat next to Janie. Janie gradually began answering the school psychologist's questions by shaking her head. However, she still did not communicate verbally or make eye contact with the school psychologist. She continued to visit but placed few demands on Janie; she reinforced Janie for the little nonverbal communication that took place and gently insisted that she would not be put off by Janie's rejections.

After additional time visiting Janie, the school psychologist one day gave her a note that had boxes for her to check off preferred activities (e.g., drawing versus writing; numbers versus listening). The school psychologist told Janie, "You could really use a friend to help find out what's bothering you. I want to know which activity you prefer, and whether you want me to come back next week. I know you don't want to talk, but maybe we can write notes." Although Janie refused to check a box, she did indicate nonverbally which activity she wanted and then allowed the school psychologist to check the corresponding box. At this point and for the first time in over a month, Janie turned her entire body toward the school psychologist. Janie responded to this format over the next several visits and began to check boxes on her own.

The school psychologist engaged Janie in drawing tasks, and Janie appeared eager to participate. She also spontaneously began to talk. She made direct eye contact and smiled as she worked. Not only did she answer the school psychologist's questions, but she offered information about herself. From this point on, Janie displayed good effort and, at times, seemed quite absorbed in tasks, despite environmental distractions. During the next several months, Janie continued to cooperate, volunteer information, and occasionally elicit the school psychologist's assistance. She finally indicated her willingness to leave the classroom, and the school psychologist administered a battery of tests, with no apparent discomfort for Janie.

Results of the school psychologist's observations and evaluation indicated that Janie had a major language-based learning disability. The school psychologist reported that Janie's avoidant behavior could have been her way of backing away from situations that required the type of language strategies in which she was deficient. The school psychologist noted that Janie's learning disability and her experiences with failure could have affected her willingness to participate in class as well as her interpersonal interactions.

FOCUS QUESTIONS   Why was it important for the school psychologist to establish rapport before administering a battery of tests to Janie?

What could have happened if the school psychologist had attempted to administer the tests to Janie on the first day they met?

What important professional standards for the assessment of children are illustrated by this case?

The incident illustrates a professional's care and concern about a child and respect for her well-being. Instead of immediately confronting the child with a threatening test situation that would have probably yielded invalid or no usable results, the school psychologist spent a great deal of time with Janie, getting to know her and drawing her out. The school psychologist obtained a great deal of information about Janie before meeting her and used this information to plan a strategy for working with her. Over months of working with Janie, the school psychologist obtained a wealth of clinical information. This incident is an excellent example of how good assessment practices go far beyond the actual administration of a test.

FACTORS INVOLVED

1. Comprehensive Assessment
2. Proper Test Use

ELEMENTS INVOLVED

1. Accepting responsibility for competent use of the test.
10. Being alert to test takers who show passive or aggressive nonparticipation.
60. Establishing rapport with examinees to obtain accurate scores.

26 PARENTAL CONCERN ABOUT ETHNIC BIAS IN TESTING

SETTING AND APPLICATIONS

Education

INCIDENT

A first-grade boy who was having significant academic difficulties was referred for a multifactored evaluation by a multidisciplinary team. The student's mother initially refused to give permission for the evaluation until she could examine the tests that would be used with her son. The school psychologist met with the student's mother and provided an explanation about the types of assessment that would be used and the professionals who would conduct the evaluation. The school psychologist explained to the parent that the professional standard to maintain test security prohibited him from allowing the parent to examine the instruments and also explained the reasons for maintaining test security. However, the school psychologist provided generic descriptions of tasks to the mother. The school psychologist acknowledged the parent's concerns and learned that the parent was worried about the possibility of ethnic bias during the evaluation. The parent was provided with information about the properties of the specific instruments with regard to ethnic bias, and the school psychologist explained that significant consideration would be given to nonbiased, multifactored assessment in any interpretations and decisions made as the result of the evaluation. In addition, the school psychologist suggested that professionals who were of the same ethnic background as the student could conduct portions of the evaluation, if the mother felt this would be appropriate. The school psychologist concluded the conference by telling the mother that he and other members of the multidisciplinary team would explain the evaluation results and answer additional questions following her son's evaluation and that the mother would be involved in the decisions made as the result of the evaluation. As a result of this conference, the parent agreed to give permission for the evaluation.

FOCUS QUESTIONS

Why was it important to maintain test security and not allow the mother to review test items?

Without revealing the actual test items, how could the school psychologist provide the parent with information about her son's assessment and the types of items that appear on the tests?

Why was it important for the school psychologist to address the mother's concern about her son's assessment?

This incident illustrates a professional's maintenance of test security in an educational setting, as well as his demonstration of respect for the student and his mother in this exchange. The school psychologist responded to a distressed parent's demand to examine test materials by meeting with the parent and disclosing as much information about the planned assessment as was appropriate, including the types of assessment (e.g., assessment domains such as intelligence, school achievement, and visual–motor skills), methods of assessment (e.g., norm-referenced tests, behavioral observations), the names of tests, and generic descriptions of types of items found on the tests. The school psychologist also provided an explanation to the parent about his professional commitment to maintaining test security.

This incident also illustrates that sometimes a request to disclose test items relates to a broader concern such as test bias. Upon learning of the parent's concern about test bias, the school psychologist was able to respond by providing information about tests and test bias. Although nonbiased assessment encompasses much more than administration of a test by someone of the same ethnic background, the school psychologist further acknowledged and responded to the parent's concerns by suggesting the involvement of professionals who were of the same ethnic background.

FACTORS INVOLVED

2. Proper Test Use
4. Maintaining Integrity of Test Results
7. Interpretive Feedback

ELEMENTS INVOLVED

11. Preventing individuals from reviewing actual tests prior to administration.
12. Keeping scoring keys and test materials secure.
68. Selecting tests that are as free from discrimination as possible, considering the standardization sample and the test-taker population.
71. Willingness to give interpretation and guidance to test takers in counseling situations.

27 THE FAILING FACULTY

Employment

Carl, a staff member at a community college, was asked by a local school district to recommend a test to evaluate teacher competency. His background was primarily in counseling, and he lacked formal training and experience in the use of tests for personnel selection and clarification. He suggested the Wesman Personnel Classification Test, which the manual indicated measured verbal and numerical skills. When asked about a passing score, Carl recommended a score of 70%. His decision was based partly on his belief that such a score would seem reasonable to the public because that level of performance was typically expected of school children on their exams.

According to the norms provided in the manual, a Verbal score of 70% was at the 76th percentile for salaried workers. A score of 70% on the Numeric scale was also at the 76th percentile for salaried workers. By Carl's logic, these scores became the minimally acceptable performance for teachers in the district.

About half of the teachers and an even larger proportion of principals failed. These results appeared in the local press and led to a public relations disaster for the school system.

What general approach should be followed by individuals or groups who intend to evaluate individual competency?

What factors should be considered in establishing cut-off scores on any test?

There are many examples of test misuse evident in this case. However, the primary issue is that the test user lacked the training needed for this work.

The Wesman has been successfully used for many years in the industrial–organizational area. On the other hand, Carl appeared to be unaware of critical reviews that have questioned its applicability for testing teacher competence in particular (e.g., Fruchter, 1985). Evaluating teacher competency may well prove to be a legitimate use of the Wesman. However, this will be known only through research that addresses this particular application of the Wesman.

The political fallout from the incident might have been avoided had Carl chosen a more defensible cut-off score. However, this misses the point of the case. Carl was not specifically trained in the use of tests for selection and classification. Personnel selection and classification is a specialized area that requires not only skills in testing and research design but also knowledge of federal and state hiring guidelines and policies. Setting cut scores is a value judgment that requires both technical and political sophistication.

FACTORS INVOLVED

1. Comprehensive Assessment
2. Proper Test Use
3. Psychometric Knowledge
6. Appropriate Use of Norms

ELEMENTS INVOLVED

1. Accepting responsibility for competent use of the test.
5. Knowledge of legal standards.
17. Knowledge of the test and its limitations.
25. Understanding norms and their limitations.
34. Considering whether the reason for giving a test locally meets the purpose for which the test was designed.
46. Interpreting test results properly for the particular group tested, keeping in mind the characteristics of that group.
59. Not assuming that a norm for one job applies to a different job (and not assuming that norms for one group automatically apply to other groups).
67. Selecting tests appropriate to both the purpose of measurement and to the test takers.

Section 3

Test Selection

28 USING THE WRONG CUT SCORE FROM THE WRONG TEST

SETTING AND
APPLICATIONS
Education

INCIDENT
A private vocational–technical school applied for and received a federal grant to train under- or unemployed disadvantaged youth and adults for entry-level positions in local industry. The program was designed to enable the trainees to read and comprehend technical manuals, understand and use measurement instruments such as calipers and micrometers, check the accuracy of machine set-ups, and write inspection reports.

One of the requirements in the funding contract stated that at least 65% of the trainees had to complete the program in order for the school to be paid the final installments on the per capita training allowance that it received. This requirement was included to prevent programs such as this one from collecting an allowance for enrolling applicants who had little chance of completing the training and who would subsequently drop out.

Trainees were required to have a high school diploma or equivalent for entry into the program. Based on past experience, the program administrators decided that a preliminary "crash" educational component of about 6 weeks' duration was necessary to adequately prepare the trainees. This component included technical reading comprehension, blueprint reading, and report writing. This component was included in the approved training plan.

To screen for potential dropouts, the school required that each applicant achieve a minimum cut score on the relevant subtests of the American College Testing Assessment (ACT), which was administered at a nearby ACT-designated testing center. The program administrators realized that setting a cut score too high would result in the acceptance of too few applicants into the program. To counter this possibility, they set the cut score so low that it fell within the range of scores that could be achieved simply by random marking on the ACT exam answer sheet. As it turned out, the school indeed had a higher dropout rate for the academic component of the program than that permitted under the contract.

FOCUS
QUESTIONS
Outline a plan for constructing a criterion-referenced admissions test for the training program.

Given the nature of the program offered by the vocational–technical school, and the population that it served, what kind of information other than test scores could be collected as part of a screening procedure that could be used to identify potential dropouts?

What is the ACT designed to measure, and how useful is it in screening for potential dropouts in this program?

What factors should the program administrators consider when setting a cut-off score?

The vocational school might be commended for its efforts to reduce the dropout rate of a population with special needs and for its concern that the cut score not be too high and thus eliminate the very applicants the program was designed to serve. However, the school's admission procedures relied on the scores of a test that was not designed for this purpose nor normed on this type of population. The ACT is intended primarily as a broad measure of educational development for use with high school students. Instruments designed to measure adult reading comprehension and basic mathematics ability, referenced to the levels of basic skills needed to benefit from such training programs, would have been a better choice.

Another option would be to design a test specifically for use in this program, with demonstrable construct validity, and referenced to the level of difficulty of the instructional material used in the 6-week crash course. Scores from this pre-test could then be correlated with achievement and persistence in the course, and the school might eventually be able to establish its own cut-off bands based on data from its own students.

FACTORS INVOLVED

2. Proper Test Use
1. Comprehensive Assessment
4. Maintaining Integrity of Test Results

ELEMENTS INVOLVED

22. Knowledge of the need for multiple sources of convergent data.
24. Recognizing that although test scores are observed, knowledges, skills, abilities, and personal characteristics may be observed in performance but are only inferred from test scores.
17. Knowledge of the test and its limitations.
34. Considering whether the reason for giving a test locally meets the purpose for which the test was designed.

29 UNGUIDED REFERRAL

SETTING AND
APPLICATIONS
Speech-Language-Hearing

INCIDENT

A speech-language pathologist sent a speech and language evaluation report, dated April 10, 1990, to another speech and language clinic. The report contained a recommendation to refer a client for treatment services. The same report had been made available by the evaluator to relevant educators, medical personnel, and the parents of the client. The report contained the age level and language quotient scores for both the Utah Test of Language Development (1967) and the Zimmerman Preschool Language Scale (1969), although standard scores, standard error of measurement, and test interpretation information were lacking. Because the report was sent without a cover letter, the purpose for sending the report had to be derived from the report recommendations.

**FOCUS
QUESTIONS**

What other information might have been useful for the speech-language pathologist to provide to the reader of the report?

What resources might a speech-language pathologist use to determine if additional and perhaps more current instruments were available for use in a speech and language evaluation?

Failure to keep abreast of changes in tests and testing procedures led to the administration of a test battery with limited diagnostic capabilities. Among speech-language pathology practitioners, both administered tests are considered as screening instruments rather than diagnostic tests. Using old, unrevised versions of the Utah Test of Language Development and the Zimmerman Preschool Language Scale would make the test scores obtained suspect as would the use of outdated normative data.

Lack of current research knowledge led to the reporting of age level scores whose inadequacy has been demonstrated. Some problems with age scores are that the same absolute difference in scores may not represent the same age differences throughout the age spectrum and score differences at adjacent age levels may not be statistically significantly different from one another.

The lack of information about the purpose of the referral and of information about the clinical meaning of the data reported make the report virtually useless to another speech-language pathologist. Its use by professionals outside the field who would not have detailed knowledge about the tests and scoring could lead to unwarranted conclusions about the presence of a problem.

This is an issue particularly relevant to parents. Although parents have the right to obtain a copy of an evaluation report, sending it without discussing the contents or without altering the wording to make it intelligible to the parents is not consistent with providing the best quality clinical services.

FACTORS INVOLVED

1. Comprehensive Assessment
2. Psychometric Knowledge

ELEMENTS INVOLVED

28. Keeping up with the field and checking one's own interpretations with others.
29. Applying principles of test theory and principles of test interpretation.
86. Refraining from reporting scores to administrators without adequate interpretation.
20. Considering errors of measurement of a test score.
41. Understanding standard scores and percentile ranks.

30 Mistaken Diagnosis

SETTING AND
APPLICATIONS
Speech-Language-Hearing

INCIDENT   Asked to decide and provide a report within 1 week about which children in a preschool group might benefit from speech and language treatment services, a speech-language pathologist reviewed her records. Because of the large number of children in the preschool, she decided not to retest any children and to use her recent test results, which she had obtained within the previous month. Different tests had been used with different children. The clinician used the results of the Boehm Test of Basic Concepts (Preschool Version) to diagnose a language disorder in a 4½-year-old preschooler. The child, of African-American heritage, lived in a low socioeconomic area of the inner city. His score of 45 placed him at the 40th percentile for his age group. This score led the clinician to diagnose that the boy had a language disorder.

FOCUS
QUESTIONS   Was the Boehm an appropriate test to administer to the child?
Was the diagnosis correct and was it warranted, based on the data presented?

ANALYSIS

Too little time for testing and too limited an array of assessment instruments for a preschool population led to inappropriate use of the Boehm Test, incorrect diagnosis of a language disorder, and use of insufficient evidence to make a diagnosis. The diagnosis of the presence of a language disorder was made on the basis of a single test, even though the test manual clearly states that an early childhood education evaluation should consist of information obtained from many sources and that the Boehm should not be used as the sole readiness or screening instrument. Furthermore, the clinician misinterpreted the test score and made an incorrect diagnosis. Performance at the 40th percentile would place the child within the range of normal. In general, performance within one standard deviation of the mean score (50th percentile for normally distributed data) is considered to be within normal limits. A score at the 40th percentile is less than one half standard deviation below the mean score.

The information that the Boehm test provides was misused. The test is designed to assess a child's understanding of relational language concepts, not to determine the presence of a language disorder. Although the Boehm has good predictive validity for classroom performance, it lacks good concurrent agreement with tests of linguistic ability. Although Boehm results could have been reported as concepts the child has mastered and concepts not mastered, these results should not have been considered as the basis for the diagnosis itself.

FACTORS INVOLVED

1. Comprehensive Assessment
2. Proper Test Use
3. Psychometric Knowledge

ELEMENTS INVOLVED

40. Refraining from making evaluations from inappropriate tests.
45. Choosing tests sufficient to sample behaviors for a specific purpose.
30. Resisting political pressures to shorten the planning, diagnostic, and interpretive process unduly.
28. Keeping up with the field and checking one's own interpretations with others.
47. Avoiding interpretation beyond the limits of the test.
23. Skill in taking a good history to integrate with test results.
3. Maintaining proper actions regardless of management pressures.
17. Knowledge of the test and its limitations.
20. Considering errors of measurement of a test score.
44. Understanding standard errors of estimate and standard errors of measurement.
25. Understanding norms and their limitations.
67. Selecting tests appropriate to both the purpose of measurement and to the test takers.

31 INSUFFICIENT ASSESSMENT

**SETTING AND
APPLICATIONS**
Neuropsychology

INCIDENT
A 31-year-old man suffered a head injury resulting from a tire explosion and causing loss of consciousness for 3 months. He had been employed as the manager of a service station for several years before the accident. Frontal lobe damage was documented by a brain scan, and the patient was referred for assessment of ability to work. The assessor administered tests of intelligence and immediate memory only. These tests produced scores in the average range. The patient denied a psychiatric history. The assessor concluded that the patient had recovered sufficiently to pursue employment.

The case was appealed by the patient's spouse, and the patient was referred to a neuropsychological laboratory for a complete workup. A note attached to the case by the caseworker stated that this patient was probably guilty of malingering because he was reported to have average intelligence but was unable to maintain employment. A thorough neuropsychological workup revealed behavioral deficits consistent with brain dysfunction that were probably responsible for the patient's severely impaired impulse control, severe organizational and planning impairment, and severe deficits in motor sequencing and sustained attention. The patient was unable to inhibit his impulsive behavior and unable to maintain employment, despite a desire to be employed. He was recommended for work in a sheltered workshop.

**FOCUS
QUESTIONS**
What harm might have come to the patient or others had the first evaluation been allowed to stand?

What kinds of additional tests would have helped in identifying the patient's deficits?

The initial assessor neglected to assess key aspects of the patient's deficits because of a lack of understanding of neuropsychological principles and theory. The incomplete assessment of the patient's clinical behavior and the failure to use the assessment tools required to reveal the patient's pattern of deficits were critical factors in the erroneous conclusions of the first assessment. Even with the limited testing done, a well-trained neuropsychologist would have identified qualitative deficits reflecting impulsivity, impaired planning ability, and poor organizing skills. This would have led to additional direct testing of these areas.

FACTOR INVOLVED

1. Comprehensive Assessment

ELEMENTS INVOLVED

45. Choosing tests sufficient to sample behaviors for a specific purpose.
22. Knowledge of the need for multiple sources of convergent data.
40. Refraining from making evaluations from inappropriate tests.
47. Avoiding interpretation beyond the limits of the test.

32 MEMORY PROBLEMS MISSED

SETTING AND APPLICATIONS   Neuropsychology

INCIDENT   A clinician was asked to evaluate a patient with complaints of memory deficits in order to rule out a progressive deteriorating condition. The clinician administered a test of immediate verbal and nonverbal memory. The clinician did not administer any other tests. The clinician concluded that the patient's memory functioning was entirely within normal limits. The clinician's errors caused the patient—who was in fact suffering from a chronic deteriorating condition—to be denied timely treatment.

FOCUS QUESTION   What other types of tests should the clinician have administered?

The clinician should have assessed memory more fully by, at the minimum, examining delayed memory. In addition, tests should have been administered to determine if the patient had difficulty with recall, cued recall, or recognition. The patient's verbal and nonverbal learning, semantic relations, calculations, and constructions should also have been assessed. The clinician in this case showed a lack of knowledge of important principles of brain functioning and the measurement of brain functioning.

Despite the specificity of the referral question, the clinician should also have assessed other cognitive skills (e.g., language, spatial, attentional, and executive functions) that can be impaired as a result of a progressive deteriorating condition. Emotional status also should have been examined.

FACTOR INVOLVED

1. Comprehensive Assessment

ELEMENTS INVOLVED

23. Skill in taking a good history to integrate with test results.
45. Choosing tests sufficient to sample behaviors for a specific purpose.
22. Knowledge of the need for multiple sources of convergent data.

Section 4

Test Administration

33 STANDARDIZED TESTING CONDITIONS

SETTING AND APPLICATIONS

Employment

INCIDENT

As part of its selection process, a company administered a standardized typing test to all secretarial applicants. The score was the number of words correctly typed per minute. Errors lowered the score.

Clerical assistants administered the test in the personnel office. Although all applicants used the same machine, the keyboard contained an unusual number of special keys that displaced some of the standard keys. It was not typical of most machines in use by the company and therefore was regularly available for use in testing. The unusual keyboard tended to penalize good typists who rarely needed to look at the keyboard. Those who passed the test were often typists with limited training and experience.

In addition, the clerical assistants often administered the test while they were involved in other activities. They paid little attention to the applicants. Some applied the time limits rigidly. Others stopped applicants when they came to a stopping place in their own work.

FOCUS QUESTIONS

What steps might be taken to ensure that the typing test is administered properly and fairly to all applicants?

What other testing might be added to the process to supplement the information derived from the typing test?

A test score is useful for employment selection when it accurately samples the kinds of behaviors used on the job. The need for exactly standardized equipment when testing motor tasks cannot be overemphasized. If the use of specific apparatus is an essential element of the test or job, assessment with other kinds of apparatus may give very misleading results. In this case, the kind of machine used made the task very different from what would be encountered on the job itself. Besides being unfair to applicants, the procedure is unfair to the organization: Qualified applicants and the contributions that they can make are lost to the company.

Organizations that test extensively often rely on multiple test administrators. When this happens, each administrator must be properly and uniformly instructed by those in charge of the testing program to ensure uniformity in the testing process and fairness to examinees. This is true not only in industrial settings but in educational and certification settings also. Large-scale assessment programs that conduct testing at many different sites need to provide test proctors with clear manuals, training, and procedures for handling irregularities that may occur during the testing process.

Because some aspects of job performance are more clearly "testable," there is a tendency to rely on those indicators more heavily than is always warranted. The facts in this regard are not available in this case. Nevertheless, a valid and uniformly administered typing test may sample only a small fraction of the activities required by the job. Logical thinking, comprehension of business information, and contact skills also may play an important part in differentiating those who are successful on the job from those who are not. A careful job analysis helps ensure that all important elements will be identified prior to the design and implementation of any testing program.

FACTOR INVOLVED

2. Proper Test Use

ELEMENTS INVOLVED

61. Seeing that every examinee follows directions so that test scores are accurate.
63. Following timing instructions accurately, especially for short speeded tests.
65. Giving standard directions as prescribed.
17. Knowledge of the test and its limitations.
15. Restricting test administration to qualified personnel.

34 STANDARDIZED ADMINISTRATION PROCEDURES

SETTING AND APPLICATIONS

Counseling/Training

INCIDENT

A nonprofit vocational rehabilitation agency used test results along with interview and other sources of data to suggest areas of vocational training for each of its clients. Although the testing was typically conducted by the staff psychometrist, a staff counselor administered Form B of the General Aptitude Test Battery (GATB) to a small group of adults with physical disabilities on a day on which the psychometrist was ill. Each of the individuals in this group was in a wheelchair, having lost one or both legs. After following the standard directions for administering the finger dexterity test, a timed test that includes a prescribed demonstration of placing washers on rivets, the counselor started the timer.

After 30 seconds had elapsed, the counselor noticed that most of the clients were having extreme difficulty with the test materials and realized that his demonstration had been incorrect. He stopped the test, instructed the clients not to change any of the items they had already completed, repeated the directions, and demonstrated the proper sequence of manipulation of the rivets. He then restarted the test from that point after subtracting the time that had already elapsed from the remaining test time.

The tests were then scored on the regular adult norms, and individual Occupational Aptitude Patterns were calculated according to the standard procedure. Because the test data were only to be used as a counseling tool and not as a barrier or gateway to vocational training, the counselor saw no need to report the irregularity in the administration of the subtest. Its results were entered into the clients' records "as is," along with the other subtest scores and the Occupational Aptitude Patterns.

FOCUS QUESTIONS

What are the pros and cons of administering standardized tests to persons with disabilities? If tests are administered, what factors must be considered when selecting the test? When administering the test? When interpreting the test?

The use of standardized tests can sometimes help expand career opportunities for persons with disabilities by identifying their particular strengths. Tests should only be used, however, if there is a reasonable chance that the results can help the individual select a job or career. Also, a test should not be administered to an individual if it is likely to cause distress for the individual. The test administrator should be sensitive to any test items that may be unduly difficult for, or upsetting to, the person with a disability. Also, when interpreting the test results, the professional should consider whether or not the disabled individual is likely to perform better on the job than on the test. Test items are designed to be samples of job-related behavior. An individual's response to the items is therefore believed to be generalizable to the behaviors required on the job. Some individuals with disabilities may, however, have learned atypical but entirely successful behaviors that can be applied to the performance of job-related tasks. These behaviors may not be represented by any of the standard test items.

Use of the particular test in this case (GATB) and scoring it on standard norms with a population of adults having certain physical disabilities may be appropriate. However, some comment should have been entered onto the test record regarding the nature of each individual's physical condition and its possible effect, if any, on the motor test scores.

A number of factors in the testing situation described here may have caused additional problems. Note that these comments are applicable whether or not the individuals taking the test had disabilities.

If test results are to yield useful information, they must be properly administered. Since it was not his regular assignment, the counselor should have practiced the test administration procedure until he was proficient before he began an actual administration. Alternatively, the testing could have been rescheduled to a date when an experienced test administrator was available.

Restarting an interrupted session in which timing is critical may have resulted in spuriously low scores for some, or all, of the clients. A better approach might have been to restart the dexterity test from the beginning with the rivets and washers in their normal starting arrangement.

Finally, some notation should have been made of the irregularity of the testing procedures on the clients' records. This is particularly crucial on the GATB because of the use of thresholds or cut scores that are used in calculating the Occupational Aptitude Patterns.

1. Comprehensive Assessment
2. Proper Test Use
3. Psychometric Knowledge
4. Maintaining Integrity of Test Results

78. Referring to a test as a basis for an interpretation only when the test has been properly administered and scored and the interpretation is well validated.
1. Accepting responsibility for competent use of the test.
8. Providing appropriate training and quality control over operations for all users of tests and test results.
15. Restricting test administration to qualified personnel.
33. Taking into account conditions that cast doubt on using reported validity for a local situation.
65. Giving standard directions as prescribed.

35 INTELLECTUAL ASSESSMENT OF A BILINGUAL STUDENT

SETTING AND APPLICATIONS

Education

INCIDENT

Juan G.'s parents, Mexican migrant laborers with valid green cards, decided to stay on after the harvest in a southeastern city close to the town where they had found summer work. Thirteen-year-old Juan enrolled in the local middle school, where he was placed in an English as a Second Language (ESL) class. After several weeks' time, Juan's teacher noticed that he seemed deficient in all language skills when compared with other students whose dominant language was Spanish. The teacher indicated that Juan seemed particularly weak in listening comprehension and speaking and referred Juan to the school's multidisciplinary team in order to determine whether Juan could benefit from the services offered in the special education program.

The multidisciplinary team recommended that the school psychologist administer an intelligence test to Juan. The psychologist, who had an undergraduate minor in Spanish and was fluent in the language, administered an experimental Spanish edition of the Wechsler Intelligence Scale for Children–Revised (WISC-R) because no other more appropriate instrument was available. Since Juan seemed to have difficulty understanding the directions on several of the verbal and nonverbal subtests of the Spanish version of the WISC-R, the examiner often stopped the timing on items, repeated directions, and resumed the timing when it appeared that Juan understood the directions. Because norms were not available for the Spanish version, the psychologist obtained subtest scaled scores and IQs using the norms for the corresponding English edition. She felt justified in using the English edition norms because she knew that the English edition had been carefully translated into Spanish and then independently translated back into English, with careful attention given to the resolution of discrepancies arising from translation.

The psychologist's administration of the experimental Spanish version of the WISC-R was the only type of assessment conducted for Juan. Because the WISC-R IQs were all 75 or slightly higher, the multidisciplinary team determined that Juan was not eligible for the special education program and recommended that Juan receive intensive remediation in basic skills in the ESL class.

No further evaluation was recommended by the multidisciplinary team. Juan's IQ scores were entered along with the team's recommendation on Juan's permanent record, with no additional comment or explanation about the nature of the scores.

FOCUS QUESTIONS

What cautions should the examiner have used in the selection, administration, and interpretation of the experimental Spanish edition of the WISC-R for Juan?

What other types of assessment information should have been collected by the multidisciplinary team to make placement decisions and plan interventions for Juan?

The incident illustrates several inappropriate assessment practices. First, the administration procedures used with the experimental Spanish version of the WISC-R did not follow standardized directions. The test should not have been interrupted and restarted after the directions were repeated. Instead, the examiner should have carefully observed the student's performance on the practice items before proceeding with the subtest. Second, despite the careful translation of the WISC-R into Spanish, the English edition norms cannot be used to interpret performance on the Spanish translation unless the two editions have been statistically equated. Such equivalence studies are difficult to execute in practice. The examiner should definitely not have entered test scores of doubtful validity on the student's record.

Third, examiners who conduct evaluations of Hispanic students must determine whether or not the Hispanic version of a test is applicable to the student in view of his or her background (e.g., Puerto Rican, Mexican, or Cuban). Juan's examiner should have determined that this version was inappropriate for Juan.

Fourth, a research edition of a test should never be used to make a clinical placement decision. Results from the experimental Spanish version may have been used along with other evaluative evidence to assist the multidisciplinary team with the evaluation of Juan's problems.

Finally, the multidisciplinary team made a decision about Juan using the results from only one assessment, and as a result, Juan may have been denied needed services and interventions. A multidimensional evaluation of all areas of functioning related to a problem is necessary in order to make valid decisions and to gather information for planning appropriate interventions. In Juan's case, the results of the Spanish edition of the WISC-R actually supplied very little information, and a more comprehensive evaluation was needed. For example, hearing and speech production assessment should have been included in the evaluation because Juan's classroom performance hinted that a hearing loss or speech problem might have accounted for his limited language skills. Both formal and informal assessment of Juan's listening skills and observations of Juan's classroom behavior should have been conducted. A conference with Juan's teacher should have been held to identify any specific concerns about Juan's academic skills. A conference with Juan's parents would have yielded important information about medical and health history, home behavior, any previous school problems, and any concerns they had about Juan.

1. Comprehensive Assessment
2. Proper Test Use
4. Maintaining Integrity of Test Results

13. Refraining from modifying prescribed administration procedures to adapt to particular individuals.
22. Knowledge of the need for multiple sources of convergent data.
45. Choosing tests sufficient to sample behaviors for a specific purpose.
48. Refraining from using a research version of a test without norms for a non-English-speaking group to make placement decisions for such a group.
61. Seeing that every examinee follows directions so that test scores are accurate.
86. Refraining from reporting scores to administrators without adequate interpretation.

36 THE INCOMPETENT EXAMINER

SETTING AND APPLICATIONS

Mental Health

INCIDENT

A 22-year-old woman was referred to Dr. C., a clinical psychologist. During elementary and high school, the woman had participated in a special education program for children who were educable mentally retarded. The woman had no physical or sensory disabilities. The woman left school at the age of 16 and, since that time, had been unemployed and lived with her parents. Her parents referred her to Dr. C. to obtain his assistance in making plans for her future vocational training.

Dr. C. administered an intelligence test to the woman. He used the Wechsler Adult Intelligence Scale (WAIS), instead of the newer (by 26 years) WAIS-R(evised), because he had tried the WAIS-R a couple of times and was sure that the scores seemed too low. During administration of the WAIS, Dr. C. deviated somewhat from standardized procedures because he felt that the client needed more structure. For example, when querying the client about questionable responses on the Vocabulary subtest, he used specific questions instead of the neutral queries indicated in the test manual. When the client defined "breakfast" as "food," Dr. C. asked, "Yes, but what time of day do we eat the food?" Dr. C. decided not to administer the Arithmetic subtest because his client said that she "hated math." In addition, he opted not to administer the Object Assembly because "it takes too much time with low-functioning clients." As a result of these subtest omissions, Dr. C. prorated the IQ scores.

In the report of the evaluation, Dr. C. attributed the client's low performance on the Vocabulary subtest to her "inability to express ideas in words due to unresolved neurotic conflicts." He interpreted the client's better ability on Digits Backward than on Digits Forward to "negativism." He described the client's low score on Information as a function of "repressive tendencies and poor ego functioning." Dr. C. concluded that, because the WAIS Full Scale, Verbal, and Performance IQs were all in the high 60s, the woman was mentally retarded. He recommended that she participate in a community training program for the mentally retarded.

FOCUS QUESTIONS

Are there conditions under which it is preferable to use an older version of a test (e.g., the WAIS) as opposed to a newer version (e.g., the WAIS-R)?

What other tests might Dr. C. have used to support or refute his conclusion that the young woman was mentally retarded?

The client was referred with a request for help in formulating plans for vocational training. Dr. C. administered only one test, an intelligence test, that provides very limited information relevant to vocational planning. His data were insufficient to support his recommendation that the woman participate in a community training program. More comprehensive assessment and a number of more specific recommendations were called for, given the referral question. If Dr. C. did not have the training or experience to conduct a comprehensive assessment of the woman, he should have referred her to another professional.

Competent assessment requires that assessors follow all procedures for standardized test administration, be familiar with current research and guidelines for valid use and interpretation of instruments, and conduct comprehensive, multidimensional assessments that fully address the reasons for referral. Dr. C. failed to adhere to several principles of appropriate assessment practices.

Dr. C. elected to use the WAIS instead of the WAIS-R based only on his very limited experience with the WAIS-R and his judgment that the WAIS-R scores were too low. If Dr. C. had consulted the research on differences between the two tests, he would have seen that investigators have concluded that WAIS norms are out-of-date, yielding scores that are six or seven points too high by current standards. Dr. C. should not have let his experience with, and apparent comfort with, the older WAIS stand in the way of assessing the client with the most up-to-date measure available, the WAIS-R.

Dr. C. departed from standard procedures when administering the WAIS, giving the client directions beyond those allowed by the standardized instructions. Failure to follow standardized procedures invalidated the test norms in this case. In addition, Dr. C. did not administer two subtests in order to save time and avoid a possible area of weakness for the client. Neither of these rationales is compelling. Subtests should never be omitted because they may prove tedious. Moreover, all subtests should be administered unless the client has a special handicap, such as a physical disability, that prevents administration of a subtest. Prorating IQ scores is permissible if a subtest cannot be administered or the administration is somehow spoiled (e.g., by examiner error). Dr. C. should have administered all subtests and should not have prorated the IQ scores.

Dr. C. used psychodynamic concepts to interpret some of the client's low subtest scores. Psychologists have hypothesized psychodynamic influences on intelligence test performance in numerous books and articles. However, these hypotheses have not been empirically validated. At the very least, it was inappropriate for Dr. C. to make psychodynamic interpretations in the absence of strong, corroborating data from other assessment techniques. Dr. C. should review current texts and attend professional development workshops on the assessment of intelligence to learn guidelines for valid interpretations of intelligence test performance.

Dr. C. concluded that the client was mentally retarded solely on the basis of the IQ scores obtained from an improper administration of an outdated intelligence test. Deficits in adaptive behavior, as well as appropriately documented subaverage intelligence, must be substantiated before a person meets accepted criteria of mental retardation. Dr. C. gathered no information about this woman's adaptive behavior. There is not enough evidence to warrant Dr. C.'s classification of mental retardation for this woman.

1. Comprehensive Assessment
2. Proper Test Use
3. Psychometric Knowledge

1. Accepting responsibility for competent use of the test.
13. Refraining from modifying prescribed administration procedures to adapt to particular individuals.
17. Knowledge of the test and its limitations.
22. Knowledge of the need for multiple sources of convergent data.
25. Understanding norms and their limitations.
27. Appreciating the implications of test validity.
28. Keeping up with the field and checking one's own interpretations with others.
40. Refraining from making evaluations from inappropriate tests.

45. Choosing tests sufficient to sample behaviors for a specific purpose.
47. Avoiding interpretation beyond the limits of the test.
65. Giving standard directions as prescribed.
78. Referring to a test as a basis for an interpretation only when the test has been properly administered and scored and the interpretation is well validated.

37 USE OF SUBSTANDARD TESTING EQUIPMENT

SETTING AND APPLICATIONS

Speech-Language-Hearing

INCIDENT

A practicing speech-language pathologist wrote a letter complaining to the test author about the poor quality of the audiocassette that was used with the administration of the Goldman-Fristoe-Woodcock Test of Auditory Discrimination (G-F-W). This test requires that the auditory stimuli be presented via a high fidelity tape recording. Upon reviewing the complaint, the test author requested that the taped material be sent so that it could be reviewed and assessed. When the recording was received and evaluated, it was determined to be most definitely an inferior recording. It was obvious that the examiner was using a highly distorted copy of the published recording. It was no wonder that he was having difficulty with his clients' test results.

In a related case with the same test, another examiner reported a tremendous failure rate with his clients. When questioned regarding the type of equipment used, his reel-to-reel tape recorder proved adequate, but when asked about the type of earphones employed, the examiner noted that they were "high fidelity." When the earphones in question were obtained and analyzed, however, it was discovered that their frequency response was so weak above 1000 Hz that the test results were invalid.

FOCUS QUESTIONS

What types of procedures could have been used by these speech-language pathologists to assure that the equipment used was in proper operating condition?

What might the test publisher do to assure that test administrators do not use copies rather than originals of published materials?

The examiners failed to read the manual and follow the specifications for the required equipment. Also, the examiners should have used the standard high-quality tapes that are issued with the test rather than a poor copy.

In these cases, the examiners were obtaining too many false positives and were describing clients as impaired when they might not have been. This description could result in improper categorization of a client and inappropriate treatment.

These testing problems could have been avoided if the following steps had been taken:

1. The examiners should have accepted responsibility for thoroughly studying the test manuals and following the standard procedures cited.

2. The examiners could have prevented the problem by using standard procedures, audiotapes, and earphones as prescribed and by verifying the status and calibration of the equipment.

The positive factor is that the examiners realized that the results were questionable and checked with the author to remedy the situation.

2. Proper Test Use
1. Comprehensive Assessment

16. Using settings for testing that allow for optimum performance by the test takers.
1. Accepting responsibility for competent use of the test.
28. Keeping up with the field and checking one's own interpretations with others.

38 NOT LISTENING TO THE TEST AUTHOR

SETTING AND APPLICATIONS

Speech-Language-Hearing

INCIDENT

A group of audiologists was employing the Goldman-Fristoe-Woodcock Test of Auditory Discrimination (G-F-W) as a means of comparing performance with other audiometric discrimination tests. After testing a number of individuals, they reported poor performance on the G-F-W. The poor results occurred not only with individuals with hearing impairment but also with listeners with normal hearing. Upon investigation, it was noted that the audiologists failed to adhere to the standardized administration procedures outlined in the test manuals. Specifically, they were abbreviating the Picture–Word Association pretest portion of the test.

FOCUS QUESTIONS

How does the utility of test results become compromised when standardized test administration procedures are not followed?

What topics might be included in a training program for administration of the G-F-W and other tests of auditory discrimination?

The examiners failed to adhere to the test manual requirements. They did not take responsibility to ensure that they were following standard procedures. Rather than completing the designated pretest protocol, they wrongly assumed that the adults knew the appropriate picture–word associations. Although these picture–word associations were generally simple, there were a number of abstractions that subjects might have failed to recognize without the training procedures. Although the test manual clearly designated the pretraining requirement, in an attempt to reduce time of test administration, these professionals were misusing the test and obtaining inappropriate results.

Because the goal of this study was to compare tests, the results were not being used for decisions about specific clients. However, there could have been a remote adverse effect if the data had been reported and, on that basis, the validity of the G-F-W were questioned.

This problem could have been prevented if the examiners had given the test in a standard fashion as prescribed in the test manuals. The examiners should also have accepted the responsibility for studying the test procedures carefully and following the directions as outlined. Finally, the examiners should not have omitted the pretest training to save time.

FACTOR INVOLVED

2. Proper Test Use

ELEMENTS INVOLVED

65. Giving standard directions as prescribed.
1. Accepting responsibility for competent use of the test.
30. Resisting political pressures to shorten the planning, diagnostic, and interpretive process unduly.

39 TESTING PERSONS WHO ARE BLIND

SETTING AND APPLICATIONS

Employment

INCIDENT

A blind person applied to take a professional certification examination. The applicant wished to use readers and was permitted to bring her own readers as long as they were not experts in the professional field.

There was only one form of the examination, which was to be given nationwide on the same day. The examination for sighted applicants required two 3-hour sessions, one in the morning and one in the afternoon. The person who was blind was required to complete the examination on the same day. She was allowed to work from 8 a.m. until 6 p.m. and to work through lunch. She worked through lunch and only took one 10-minute break in the entire day.

This 10-hour day was tremendously fatiguing for the blind applicant. At the end of the day, she said that she could not think at all. (For this applicant, the test-taking task consisted of listening to the question, committing it to memory, reasoning through to an answer, giving the answer, then forgetting the question, and moving on to the next item.)

FOCUS QUESTIONS

In what ways could the test have been administered so that the applicant would have been best served and the test results scores would have remained valid?

What are the arguments for and against using readers who are experts in the field being examined?

The applicant was required to work under extremely fatiguing conditions, and hence, it is doubtful that her test scores were an accurate reflection of her professional knowledge. Sighted test applicants are unlikely to be required to take a test for 10 hours in 1 day. In addition, the applicant should have been given more time; studies (Nester, 1984) suggest that applicants using a reader require approximately double the usual amount of time for tests of this type.

The decision makers who administered this program based their decision about time constraints only on the fixed idea that everyone must complete the test on the same day. When testing a person with a visual disability, or any other disability, professionals should be aware of the requirements of the Rehabilitation Act of 1973, as amended in 1978, 1986, and 1987, and the Americans with Disabilities Act (ADA) of 1990. According to the ADA (Title III), examinations offered by a private entity for certification purposes must be given in a place and manner accessible to persons with disabilities. This includes modifying the examination format when necessary, such as permitting additional time. The private entity must ensure that when the examination is administered to an individual with a disability that impairs sensory, manual, or speaking skills, the examination results accurately reflect the individual's aptitude or achievement level or whatever factor the examination purports to measure, rather than the individual's impaired sensory, manual, or speaking skills (except where those skills are the factors that the examination purports to measure).

FACTORS
INVOLVED

2. Proper Test Use
1. Comprehensive Assessment

ELEMENTS
INVOLVED

5. Knowledge of legal standards.
16. Using settings for testing that allow for optimum performance by the test takers.
30. Resisting political pressures to shorten the planning, diagnostic, and interpretive process unduly.
78. Referring to a test as a basis for an interpretation only when the test has been properly administered and scored and the interpretation is well validated.

40 A CASE OF FAILURE TO COMMUNICATE

SETTING AND APPLICATIONS

Neuropsychology

INCIDENT

The Luria-Nebraska Neuropsychological Battery (LNNB) was used to evaluate a foreign national who had been in the United States less than 1 year at the time of the evaluation. The foreign national had been involved in a bar fight and sustained an injury to his head when struck by a bottle. The examiner had been contacted by an attorney who requested an evaluation to determine if the foreign national had sustained brain damage as a result of the fight. The foreign national did not speak fluent English and the examiner was not fluent in the foreign national's native tongue. Despite this language problem, the battery was administered. The examiner attempted to enhance understanding by deviating from the standard instructions and eliminating items that he believed were difficult for the examinee to understand.

FOCUS QUESTIONS

What might the examiner have done to test this individual more appropriately when he found out that the examinee was not fluent in English?

Where might the examiner have turned to obtain appropriate assistance in testing this person?

Because the examiner knew it was highly unlikely that an examiner fluent in the examinee's language could be found, he succumbed to pressure from the attorney to perform the evaluation. He performed the evaluation using the LNNB because he was not familiar with other less verbal tests that were more appropriate. The examiner's extensive deviations from standard administration procedures clearly made it inappropriate for him to compare the client's performance with that of the LNNB normative sample.

A misdiagnosis of brain injury might lead to an unneeded invasive medical diagnostic procedure that is risky to the examinee. Such a misdiagnosis would also lead to the false belief—on the part of the client and other interested parties—that the client is indeed impaired, bringing about other inappropriate consequences. For example, the client might prevail in his personal injury lawsuit, when in fact he sustained no injury.

Testing professionals must recognize their own limitations as well as the limitations of their assessment tools. The evaluation should never have been performed except under the appropriate conditions—in this case, by an examiner who could speak the examinee's language, and perhaps using other tests.

FACTORS INVOLVED

1. Comprehensive Assessment
2. Proper Test Use
3. Psychometric Knowledge

ELEMENTS INVOLVED

3. Maintaining proper actions regardless of management pressures.
13. Refraining from modifying prescribed administration procedures to adapt to particular individuals.
65. Giving standard directions as prescribed.
67. Selecting tests appropriate to both the purpose of measurement and to the test takers.
17. Knowledge of the test and its limitations.
33. Taking into account conditions that cast doubt on using reported validity for a local situation.
78. Referring to a test as a basis for an interpretation only when the test has been properly administered and scored and the interpretation is well validated.
25. Understanding norms and their limitations.

41 REASONABLE TESTING MODIFICATIONS FOR A PERSON WITH ATTENTION DEFICIT DISORDER

SETTING AND APPLICATIONS

Employment

INCIDENT

A young woman with an attention deficit disorder completed her teacher training program in special education and applied to take the teacher certification test used in her state. When she did not pass the Communications Skills test covering listening, reading, and writing, she applied for a retest in a special administration with extra testing time. Her request was granted, but even with extra time, she did not reach the score used as the cut-off necessary for certification in her state. When she failed a second attempt with extra testing time, she applied to take the test with unlimited time and the opportunity to discuss the test questions and her answers with the test administrator. The basis for her request was that she had often been given final examinations orally in her teacher training program and that her attention deficit disorder prevented her being able to input, integrate, and output information at a normal rate for her age and intelligence. The State Education Agency (SEA), in consultation with the private testing company, denied her request on the basis that such modifications would so change the examination that it would not test the communication skills required on the job.

FOCUS QUESTIONS

What are the criteria for determining what reasonable modifications in testing practices, policies, or procedures are necessary to avoid discriminating against a test taker on the basis of disability?

What are the legal requirements of testing administrators with respect to modifying testing policies, practices, or procedures for persons with disabilities?

The first issue to consider is whether this young woman is covered by the Americans with Disabilities Act (ADA) of 1990. The ADA has broad implications for the testing of persons with disabilities. The ADA definition of a person with a disability includes individuals who have a record of a physical or mental impairment that substantially limits one or more major life activities. Because she has a record of an attention deficit disorder, this woman probably would be covered by the ADA.

Section 504 of the Rehabilitation Act of 1973 and the ADA apply to the testing conditions for this woman. An SEA, as a recipient of federal grants, is covered by Section 504. Both Section 504 and the ADA require reasonable modifications in the testing of people with disabilities, and it is necessary to consider both the status of the entity administering the test and the purpose of the test. Because both the SEA (a public entity) and a private testing company (a private entity) are involved in the testing, both Title III and Title II of the ADA apply. Title II (effective January 26, 1992) prohibits a public entity, namely, a state or local government agency, from discriminating against qualified individuals with disabilities on the basis of disability in the granting of licenses or certification. Title III (also effective January 26, 1992) requires private testing entities to offer the following to test takers with disabilities: testing in an accessible place and manner or alternative accessible arrangement; examination selection and administration to accurately reflect the individual's aptitude or achievement level, rather than reflecting the individual's sensory, manual, or speaking impairment; changes in the length of time permitted to complete the examination or adaptation of the manner in which the examination is given, when necessary; and provision of auxiliary aids and services when necessary, unless offering such would fundamentally alter the measurement of the skills or knowledge the examination is intended to test or would result in an undue burden.

The main purpose of tests for teacher certification is to assure the minimum competency of individuals licensed to teach children. Teachers must be able to comprehend oral communication by students and be able to provide quick verbal responses to their questions. A disabled individual who, after being given reasonable testing modifications, cannot meet certification requirements that test whether he or she can perform the essential functions of the job is probably not an "otherwise qualified handicapped person" under the existing laws and should not be certified to teach.

The testing company thought that the modifications originally offered to this test taker were reasonable. Although the company had provided reasonable modifications for test takers with many kinds of disabilities and approved the request for extra testing time for this individual, it had never before had a request for such extensive modifications and did not view them as reasonable. The company believed that there could be no standardization possible if discussions of questions and answers were allowed as a modification to standardized testing and expressed its concern to the state. Under the law, a company is not required to provide aids if the aids would "fundamentally alter the measurement of the skills or knowledge the examination is intended to test."

The SEA had already established that the modification of extra time was reasonable. However, it was concerned about the effect on teaching ability of a disability so severe as to (a) prevent passing the Communications Skills test at a minimal level given extra time and (b) require the discussion of questions and answers for complete understanding of the topic. Another form of accommodation available to the agency, and one that they did not select, was to waive the requirement of taking and passing the examination.

In the real case upon which the present discussion is based, the test taker filed suit under Section 504 of the Rehabilitation Act of 1973. (The events predated the passage of the ADA.) The district court judge found that the test taker was not minimally qualified as a teacher and, therefore, she was not the "otherwise qualified handicapped person" protected under that law. Upon appeal, in *Pandazides v. Virginia Board of Education, 946 F.2d 345 (4th Cir. 1991)*, the appellate court found that the district court had erred in concluding that the teacher with a learning disability was not "otherwise qualified." The appellate court stated that the trial court had to do more than simply determine whether the teacher met all stipulated requirements of the Board of Education; it had to look to the actual requirements of the particular position being sought. The appellate court held that two factual determinations were required to answer the question of "otherwise qualified":

(a) whether the teacher could perform the essential functions of a schoolteacher and (b) whether the requirements imposed by the board actually measured those functions. Moreover, the appellate court held that, even if the lower court were to determine that the teacher could not perform her duties, it would have to determine whether modifications could be made to allow her to teach in any event. The case was returned, or remanded, to the district court. After conducting the two-step inquiry required by the appellate court, the district court again ruled against the teacher-applicant.

It is important to note that the judgment of the appellate court in this case represents one judicial circuit court's interpretation only. Other judicial circuits' interpretation of Section 504 may differ.

FACTOR INVOLVED

2. Proper Test Use

ELEMENTS INVOLVED

5. Knowledge of legal standards.
2. Knowledge of professional ethics.
67. Selecting tests appropriate to both the purpose of measurement and to the test takers.

42 Passing the Bar Examination With a Learning Disability

SETTING AND
APPLICATIONS
Employment

INCIDENT

In 1988, 32-year-old Edward had failed his bar examination twice. On the third attempt, he applied for a special test administration, which would give him extra time. He submitted documentation of a newly diagnosed learning disability. Kevin, a law student with a long history of accommodation for a learning disability, also applied for special accommodation for his first attempt at the bar examination. Both were offered time-and-a-half for taking their examinations. In a different state with a different policy, John, who had a documented learning disability in elementary and high school, but who had struggled through law school without special accommodation, was refused his request for extra time for the bar examination.

FOCUS QUESTIONS

What are the criteria for determining what reasonable modifications in testing practices, policies, or procedures are necessary to avoid discriminating against a test taker on the basis of disability?

Were the policy decisions made in the two states both equitable and will they lead to valid conclusions? Furthermore, would the policy decisions be in compliance with current law?

Should Edward and Kevin have been given testing modifications based on their qualification as persons with disabilities? Was Edward's newly diagnosed disability claim a valid one? According to the Americans with Disabilities Act (ADA) of 1990, both Edward and Kevin would be covered under the ADA (Title II and Title III) as persons with disabilities and would thereby be eligible to receive modified testing procedures. (John was also covered by these two titles of ADA.) The ADA requires that persons with disabilities receive reasonable modifications in a testing situation. An individual with a record of a disability is covered under the Act, regardless of when the disability was first recorded. Examiners may require evidence that an applicant is entitled to modifications or aids, but requests for documentation must be reasonable and must be limited to the need for the modification or aid requested.

Edward had demonstrated throughout his educational career that he could perform without special modification. Edward had never received any kind of educational or testing modifications for his disability; indeed, he did not even know he had a disability until he tried to find an explanation for his failure of the bar examination. By examining the documentation of the learning disability from a professional with expertise in diagnosing learning disabilities, it can be seen that Edward's disability was shown to be less severe than Kevin's. It could not be proved that the newly documented learning disability was responsible for the first two failures on the bar examination. However, Edward's newly diagnosed learning disability was not a less credible claim to receive modified testing practices and procedures than Kevin's long-standing diagnosis.

Kevin had a long-standing history of having been identified as a person with a disability. He would be covered under the ADA because he both has a documented record of a disability and has been regarded as an individual with a disability. Kevin was identified as having a disability while he was in first grade. He had been in special education in elementary school and in a private school with special tutoring for his secondary education. He attended a small college with a Program of Assistance in Learning especially for students with learning disabilities. In law school he was allowed extra time for his examinations. Kevin was relatively slow at reading and writing, but his motivation to perform well was extremely high. He used a computer for word processing, used spell-check software to proof his work, and revised his material until he was satisfied he had done the best he could.

John's early educational experiences were similar to Kevin's, but by the time he was in law school, he had internalized the practices he knew could help him compete. He hated admitting he had a disability and struggled hard to get by. He had little or no social life because he devoted all his time and attention to succeeding in law school. He applied for special modifications on the bar examination because he knew he could not keep pace with the other examinees over the days of required testing. In John's state at the time, extra examination time was seldom permitted, especially if such accommodations had not been permitted in law school. With the passage of the ADA, John, who had a documented learning disability, would then be eligible to receive testing modifications.

Because of differing policies in different states, the Board of Managers of the National Conference of Bar Examiners adopted a statement on considerations in testing candidates with disabilities. Published in *The Bar Examiner* (February 1991), the recommendation suggests:

- time-and-a-half as a routine policy if documentation of past accommodation exists, double time in severe cases where documentation warrants it and
- individually determined amounts of extra time where no past documentation exists.

With the passage of the ADA, individual state practices are now superseded. Of particular importance in the ADA is that modifications should be determined to meet individual needs. The focus should be on the examination's measurement of the individual test taker's skill or aptitude. The entity offering the examination must assure that the examination accurately reflects an individual's aptitude or achievement level or other factor the examination purports to measure rather than any impaired sensory, manual, or speaking skills. Therefore, for these three test takers, it needs to be determined on an individual basis that additional time is the appropriate modification. Furthermore, if additional time is viewed as the appropriate modification, the amount of time should also be determined on an individual basis.

FACTOR INVOLVED	2. Proper Test Use
ELEMENTS INVOLVED	5. Knowledge of legal standards. 2. Knowledge of professional ethics.

43 TESTING INDIVIDUALS WITH PHYSICAL DISABILITIES

SETTING AND APPLICATIONS

Education

INCIDENT

Three individuals with physical disabilities as a result of cerebral palsy—Karen, Paul, and Judy—were students in three different high schools whose college-bound seniors were scheduled to take their college admissions tests on a Saturday morning in March.

Karen, whose physical disability was of mild severity, had been in special education classes only during her early school years. She seldom needed any special help because of her disability and she went ahead and registered to take her test along with the rest of her class. On the day of the test, she found herself working less and less efficiently under the time pressure because of physical fatigue, but she believed that she had probably done a fairly good job overall.

Paul had been in special education for all of his school career. He was somewhat slow at getting his work accomplished primarily because of his disability. Nevertheless, he had earned average grades, and his counselor helped him to register for the test along with the rest of the seniors in his school. On the day of the test, he answered only one half to two thirds of the questions in each of the six test sections. He felt devastated at the end of the testing period.

Judy used a wheelchair for mobility and was used to having extra testing time in her mainstream classes in high school. Her counselor helped arrange for a special test administration for Judy during the week following the Saturday test date. Judy was allowed to skip her Thursday classes and take the test in a one-on-one administration, proctored by her counselor. On the test date, Judy was placed at a table in the counselor's outer office, given the test and the standard instructions, and told to start working. During the day, students came and went from the counselor's office; conversations disturbed Judy's concentration; and the counselor checked her only occasionally. Judy asked a student to bring her a carton of milk for lunch so that she could keep working through the lunch hour. Her counselor, seeing Judy thanking the student for the milk, scolded her for talking during the test. Judy explained the situation but was in tears because of the incident. Nevertheless, she finished the test before school was over, and she hoped her scores would be good enough to allow her to attend the state university.

FOCUS QUESTIONS

What types of testing modifications for individuals with physical disabilities should be considered and what are the criteria that should determine these modifications?

What are the responsibilities of counselors with regard to testing people with disabilities?

People with disabilities are protected by federal legislation in the testing situation. For example, the Americans with Disabilities Act (ADA) of 1990 specifies that persons with disabilities are eligible for modifications in testing policies. Although the presence of a disability may not necessitate a special test modification, a person with a disability as defined by the Act is eligible to request modifications. Modifications have to be made, however, only when people request them. People with disabilities are not required to participate in separate programs such as special test administrations, and many people with disabilities take standard administrations of standardized tests. However, if persons with disabilities do not participate in separate programs, they may not receive the services they need. Title III of the ADA applies to Karen, Paul, and Judy because the company administering the test was a private entity. Title II does not apply because the school—a public entity (state or local government agency)—did not administer the test.

Karen became tired over the testing period, as do many test takers without disabilities. In Karen's case, she does have a documented disability and is covered under the ADA. If testing modifications had been provided, there would be no question of whether her disability had compromised her performance. Modifying the testing procedures to accommodate her physical fatigue would have ensured that her test scores accurately reflected her aptitude rather than her disability.

Paul clearly should have been advised by his counselor to request a special test administration. He had a documented disability and a history of need for special modifications. He was certainly eligible for them and his request would have been granted. Because the school was not the entity administering the test, the counselor may not have had a direct legal duty to advise Paul of his right to receive a special test administration. However, because the counselor knew of Paul's disability and his history of needing special modifications, the counselor had the professional responsibility of advising Paul of his right to request special modifications. Professionals should anticipate the need for special modifications and advise their clients appropriately.

Judy's test administrator also failed to provide appropriate alternative testing arrangements. She positioned Judy in an inappropriate test environment. She failed to administer the test according to standards. Her scolding of Judy was a direct result of her own failings in the situation.

Under the ADA, although testing modifications had been provided in the third case, they would have been viewed as insufficient. The ADA requires that comparable conditions be provided when alternative accessible arrangements are made.

The validity of the test scores for Paul and Judy are in question because of the failure of their counselors to provide a test environment in which these students' abilities rather than disabilities were tested.

2. Proper Test Use
1. Comprehensive Assessment

5. Knowledge of legal standards.
2. Knowledge of professional ethics.
1. Accepting responsibility for competent use of the test.
16. Using settings for testing that allow for optimum performance by the test takers.
60. Establishing rapport with examinees to obtain accurate scores.

Section 5

Test Scoring and Norms

44 PITFALLS IN COMPARING SCORES ON OLD AND NEW EDITIONS OF A TEST

SETTING AND APPLICATIONS

Education

INCIDENT

For several years, an assessment specialist in an urban school district had used the Peabody Individual Achievement Test (PIAT) as a pretest and posttest for pupils referred for special reading and mathematics instructional programs.

After administering the PIAT as a pretest near the beginning of the school year, the assessment specialist ordered PIAT-R (the revised edition of the PIAT) and decided to administer it as the posttest near the end of the year. The general drop in scores on PIAT-R compared with the original PIAT caused the assessment specialist to question the accuracy of the PIAT-R scores. Results obtained for three students (Katy, Tom, and Daniel) are shown in Table 1:

Table 1. *Comparison of PIAT and PIAT-R Results for Three Students*

Student	Age	PIAT (Pretest)		PIAT-R (Posttest)	
		Math	Reading	Math	Reading
Katy	6-9[a]	124/95[b]	119/90	113/81	111/77
Tom	11-6	101/53	107/68	93/40	100/50
Daniel	14-8	105/63	109/73	97/42	101/53

[a]Ages are shown in years and months (i.e., 6-9 means 6 years, 9 months).
[b]Values represent Standard score/percentile rank.

The assessment specialist was very puzzled by these results and subsequently expressed her lack of confidence in the PIAT-R. When neither district administrative personnel nor faculty members at a nearby university could offer a reasonable explanation for these results, the assessment specialist decided to return the PIAT-R to the publisher and use a competing achievement test because the drop in scores on PIAT-R seemed to reflect some error the publisher had made in the standardization and norming procedures.

FOCUS QUESTIONS

What did the assessment specialist overlook in placing blame on the publisher for what appeared to be a serious error?
Why can't successive editions of a test be expected to yield similar results?
What is the proper procedure for comparing scores obtained on successive editions of a test?
What procedure should the assessment specialist have followed in order to compare the scores?

ANALYSIS   The problem in the interpretation of scores from the old and new editions of PIAT arose because the assessment specialist lacked technical knowledge and understanding about the proper way to compare results on two successive editions of a test. The assessment specialist did not realize that the successive editions of PIAT contained different content specifications, different items, and were normed on different samples of pupils tested about 17 years apart. In order to compare scores on successive editions of a test, a special research study must be undertaken to administer both editions of the test to the same pupils. If this is done properly, it will be possible to establish tables of equivalent scores on the two editions. These special tables can then be used to translate scores from one edition to scores on the other edition. If tables of equivalent scores are not used to make comparisons between editions, the assessment specialist will draw erroneous conclusions about gain or loss in achievement when spring results are compared with fall results. There would appear to be losses in reading and mathematics achievement when, in reality, the problem lies in comparing two different tests. Such a situation would result in much confusion, with parents blaming teachers and teachers blaming the test. Parents, teachers, and administrators would all become embroiled in needless controversy when, in fact, the results are easily explainable and actually to be expected. Users must also consider measurement error in comparing scores on successive editions. The publisher should have provided tables of equivalent scores in the manual. Failing to locate such tables or an explanation of the comparability of scores on old and new editions of the PIAT, the assessment specialist should have contacted the publisher for an explanation of the apparent discrepancies. The publisher could then have provided the appropriate tables to make the desired comparisons.

FACTORS
INVOLVED
2. Proper Test Use
4. Maintaining Integrity of Test Results
3. Psychometric Knowledge
6. Appropriate Use of Norms

ELEMENTS
INVOLVED
25. Understanding norms and their limitations.
17. Knowledge of the test and its limitations.
34. Considering whether the reason for giving a test locally meets the purpose for which the test was designed.
41. Understanding standard scores and percentile ranks.

45 ARE OBSERVED SCORE DIFFERENCES TRUSTWORTHY?

SETTING AND APPLICATIONS Education

INCIDENT A Mountain Ridge Middle School routinely administers the Nelson Reading Skills Test (NRST) in grades 5–8 in mid-September to obtain information about reading skills early in the school year and to identify pupils in need of further evaluation. The reading supervisor works with teachers to provide further assessment, diagnosis, and remediation of reading difficulties. The NRST provides measures in vocabulary, comprehension, and rate, as well as a total score. The reading supervisor reported the incident that follows.

Helen Y., a grade 5 teacher committed to a diagnostic–prescriptive instructional approach, noted the following NRST subtest scores for Michael, one of her pupils: Word Meaning—percentile rank (PR) 46, percentile band (based on ± one standard error of measurement) 39–53; Comprehension—PR 60, percentile band 43–74; and Rate—PR 31, percentile band 5–59. Based on these results, Helen recommended a remediation plan to the reading supervisor to improve Michael's reading rate.

INCIDENT B The Highland Air Force Base Lower School (grades K–5) administers the NRST in grades 3–5 each September; the transient nature of the Lower School population results in teachers' having little useful information about prior achievement of many pupils. The NRST results provide important information both for forming homogeneous reading instructional groups[1] and about the silent reading abilities of elementary grade pupils.

Dan C., a third-grade teacher, used the NRST results for his class of 24 pupils to form reading instructional groups; he used the total score (vocabulary and comprehension) PR and listed his students, highest to lowest. He then divided them into three groups of eight each, labeled "top," "middle," and "bottom," according to their scores. Dan noted the scores of the highest and lowest scoring pupils in each group as shown in Table 1.

Table 1. *NRST Total Scores for Groups at Three Levels*

	PR	PR Band	PR	PR Band
Group	Highest pupil		Lowest pupil	
Top	99	92–99	70	59–80
Middle	64	54–75	30	20–38
Bottom	28	18–37	2	1–9

Note. PR = Percentile rank.

Dan viewed these results cautiously because he observed substantial overlap in the percentile bands of several pupils, particularly those having adjacent ranks in the listing. He knew from experience that the NRST and similar tests, although helpful in planning initial instruction, are not perfect measures of student achievement, as evidenced by the percentile bandwidth corresponding to a pupil's PR. Dan knew that the groups would change once he observed firsthand their strengths and weaknesses, and he expected the groups to continue to change as earlier needs were met and new ones arose.

FOCUS QUESTIONS What are the appropriate and inappropriate ways to interpret test scores illustrated in Incidents A and B?
What steps could a school district take to help teachers avoid making the mistakes in test score interpretation illustrated here?

---

[1] Homogeneous grouping is a controversial instructional practice that may or may not meet the needs of certain pupils. This case was not meant to introduce a debate on the merits of homogeneous or heterogeneous grouping but rather to describe the manner in which one school had used test results to implement an established instructional policy.

Both Incidents A and B deal with the necessity of recognizing the importance of measurement error in test interpretation. There is, however, a marked contrast in the way the two teachers interpreted performance on the NRST. In Incident A, the teacher did not really understand that the percentile bands are provided for the NRST and many other tests to take account of measurement error—something present in all tests. She failed to recognize that because all three percentile bands overlapped a bit, she could not conclude from Michael's NRST profile that his rate of reading was really lower than his word meaning and comprehension. Additional information from other firsthand observations or other sources would have helped confirm or refute the test scores. Although it probably would not have affected Michael adversely if the teacher had attempted to increase his rate of reading, the teacher might find her time better spent in helping other pupils in greater need of her assistance.

In Incident B, Dan C. recognized that the NRST scores provided a way to group pupils initially for instruction; however, due to measurement error present in all test scores, there was likely to be some overlap in skills among the three groups as reflected by the overlapping percentile bands of students assigned to adjacent groups. Dan realized that this skill overlap was inevitable as a result of the imperfect nature of the test scores and that he would need to remain flexible and change the groups somewhat as more information about pupil strengths and weaknesses became available from firsthand observation.

FACTOR INVOLVED

3. Psychometric Knowledge

ELEMENTS INVOLVED

20. Considering errors of measurement of a test score.
41. Understanding standard scores and percentile ranks.
50. Interpreting differences among scores in terms of the standard error concept.
25. Understanding norms and their limitations.

46 USE OF INAPPROPRIATE NORMS

SETTING AND APPLICATIONS

Neuropsychology

INCIDENT

A psychologist was asked to evaluate a 75-year-old man's cognitive status because his wife had noticed deterioration in his memory. The psychologist examined the man using a mental status exam and an intelligence test. The psychologist concluded that the patient's performance on the mental status exam was within the normal range. However, the assessor concluded the man's spatial and rapid information processing scores on the intelligence test were impaired relative to several verbal scores. He interpreted this pattern as reflecting deterioration of the man's mental functioning. The assessor did not use norms for the intelligence test that were appropriate considering the patient's age. Emotional status was not assessed. After a series of costly medical examinations to determine the cause of the purported deterioration, as well as a neuropsychological evaluation, it was concluded that the man was a perfectly healthy 75-year-old man.

FOCUS QUESTIONS

How might the man's test scores be affected by using norms more appropriate for his age? What are some reasons why the man's emotional status should have been evaluated?

ANALYSIS   The assessor used general population norms rather than age-appropriate norms to interpret differences among subtests on the intelligence test. The assessor's conclusions were inappropriate because there is a considerable body of evidence suggesting that scores on spatial and rapid information processing tests are more affected by the normal aging process than are scores on other tests of cognitive functioning. As a result, the assessor drew the wrong conclusion about the patient's functioning. Given the referral question, the assessor was also remiss in not administering a memory test. Furthermore, because depression is a common explanation for memory complaints, the man's emotional status should have been assessed. The assessor's errors caused the patient and his insurance company to pay for further evaluations that were in fact unnecessary. Concern that he might be suffering from a serious disease also caused the man and his wife considerable unnecessary emotional distress.

FACTORS
INVOLVED
1. Comprehensive Assessment
6. Appropriate Use of Norms

ELEMENTS
INVOLVED
25. Understanding norms and their limitations.
35. Recognizing, in a clinical setting, when a patient's state has been misdiagnosed or has changed, and selecting suitable norms.
45. Choosing tests sufficient to sample behaviors for a specific purpose.

Section 6

Test Interpretation

47 It's a Man's Job

SETTING AND
APPLICATIONS

Counseling/Training

INCIDENT

Barbara, a ninth-grade student, and her parents met with the high school guidance counselor to plan her program of studies for her 3 years of high school. Barbara's grades were all in the low to middle 90s (on a scale of 0 to 100), except for art, for which her grade was 80. Barbara had served as president of the school's computer science club for 2 years and had designed the computer graphics for the school's publications. During the discussion with the counselor, Barbara also expressed an interest in creative writing.

As part of the counseling arrangement, Barbara was administered the Differential Aptitude Tests (DAT) and the Kuder General Interest Survey. Her percentile scores on the DAT, based on the most recent ninth-grade female norms, were as follows: Verbal Reasoning—96; Numerical Ability—99; Verbal Reasoning + Numerical Ability—98; Abstract Reasoning—92; Space Relations—85; Mechanical Reasoning—80; Clerical Speed and Accuracy—99+; Spelling—99+; Language Usage—98. Her highest scores on the Kuder were on the Computation, Scientific, and Literary scales.

Barbara wanted to continue with college preparatory math and to study both physics and chemistry. She was also considering taking an Advanced Placement science course because she had already successfully taken a high school level biology course in the ninth grade. Because she was interested in studying either engineering or architecture in college, she wanted to substitute a mechanical drawing course for the planned fourth year of a foreign language.

The counselor pointed out to Barbara that her Space Relations and Mechanical Reasoning scores were her lowest on her DAT, which he claimed predicted "that you probably would not do as well in physics and mechanical drawing as you might in other subjects such as English and writing electives. Your aptitude scores, which predict potential success in related occupations, indicate that a career in engineering or architecture, a highly competitive male-dominated occupation, may not be realistic."

FOCUS
QUESTIONS

What kind of information would be useful in helping a student plan a course of study in high school?

Based on the information provided in the case, what other college majors might it be useful for Barbara to explore?

How might Barbara's scores on an interest inventory be incorporated into a discussion of future careers?

Should the test interpretation include a comparison of Barbara's scores to male norms? Why or why not?

TEST INTERPRETATION

As the test manual indicates, DAT results for a student of Barbara's age are as much a measure of developed abilities or achievement as they are a predictor of success in subjects considered preparatory to occupational selection. In this instance, the counselor overemphasized the importance of score differences. He was correct in pointing out that Barbara's scores on the Space Relations and Mechanical Reasoning scales were her lowest scores, relative to her other very high scores, although he failed to take into account the standard error of measurement in interpreting score differences. Her scores on these scales, however, were at or above the 80th percentile for women, levels that are appropriate for her considered career direction. The DAT manual and related literature on the test specifically advise counselors to be cautious about discouraging women from entering "male-dominated" technical fields if they score relatively poorly on Mechanical Reasoning but well on Verbal Reasoning, Numerical Ability, and other indicators. Furthermore, he should have compared Barbara's results on the DAT to male norms and explained the relevance of this procedure to her.

The best predictor of success in science and technical subjects is the combined Verbal Reasoning and Numerical Ability score. Her demonstrated interest in computer science and computer graphics and her high scores on the Scientific and Computational interest scales of the Kuder provide more information about her potential success in high school mechanical drawing courses. The counselor should have explored these other factors in counseling Barbara. In addition to the other DAT scores, her expressed interests, and her interest inventory results, information that was available about her hobbies and extracurricular activities and her grades in previous coursework should also have been incorporated into the career discussion.

In summary, the counselor relied on a narrow interpretation of test scores and did not sufficiently consider other information about Barbara's interests and academic achievement.

FACTORS
INVOLVED

1. Comprehensive Assessment
2. Psychometric Knowledge

ELEMENTS
INVOLVED

23. Skill in taking a good history to integrate with test results.
25. Understanding norms and their limitations.
32. Considering the standard error of measurement.
50. Interpreting differences among scores in terms of the standard error concept.

48 TESTING WITHOUT INTERPRETING

SETTING AND
APPLICATIONS
Employment

INCIDENT
A clinical psychologist who had a long-term consulting relationship with a large bank in the Southwest was asked by the vice president of customer services to conduct a team-building intervention in a department that had just been formed by a major reorganization of the bank. The vice president was committed to the idea that each member of the team be recognized and accepted for his or her individual strengths.

To accomplish this goal, the psychologist administered the Myers-Briggs Type Indicator (MBTI). The psychologist administered the instruments, scored them, and then handed out to each member of the department his or her own results. Although there was a general discussion of the need to appreciate differences by team members, the psychologist did not directly interpret the results of the MBTI, either individually or in the group setting. He also did not retain copies of any of the results for his files.

Following this intervention, when a new employee joined the team, the psychologist administered the MBTI and sent the results to the new staff member, without interpretation, and charged the bank for this service. This practice continued for 5 years until it came to the attention of another consultant.

FOCUS QUESTIONS
What are the dangers of handing out test results without an interpretation?
How might the MBTI, or other tests, be interpreted in a group setting? What are some of the advantages and disadvantages of group interpretations?
What kind of records should be kept of testing? Who should have access to test records?
What kind of trends would it be important to look for in testing records?

There are a number of examples of test misuse in this case. The primary misuse derives from the failure by the psychologist to provide interpretive feedback to the employees when the results were returned to them. Personality instruments, even those specifically designed to identify strengths, can easily be misinterpreted and can potentially have harmful effects if the results are misunderstood. For instance, the names of some of the MBTI scales can be confusing to a client if not properly explained because these same names (e.g., Extraversion and Introversion) have popular or even stereotypical meanings that are different from those described in the MBTI manual. Such misunderstandings could have derogatory implications for an individual and have an adverse effect on his or her self-concept if they go unaddressed. A proper interpretation of the test would include a careful explanation of the terms used to label the scales.

A proper interpretation of results can take place only in a face-to-face meeting between the client and the professional. In such a situation the interpreter can be sure that the client has adequately understood the results and can place the results in the proper perspective. This provides an opportunity for the client to ask questions to help clarify the meaning of the results. It is also the opportunity for the professional to make clear the limitations of the MBTI and of testing in general. As part of the interpretation, the consultant should also have discussed with the client what use was to be made of the MBTI results and who would have access to it.

It is also the responsibility of the consultant when working with an organization in the manner described in this case to keep a record of the results of the tests. Information about individual scores should not be made available to management of the organization, except in aggregate form (as long as the aggregates are large enough to prevent identification of any individual), or to anyone else except the individual test taker. Rather, this information should be securely stored by the consultant. Having a record of MBTI results enables the consultant to answer any questions that might occur to individuals at some later date. Keeping records on file is also the means for the consultant to evaluate the continued usefulness and appropriateness of the MBTI for use in a particular setting. There might be important trends in the data about which the organization should be informed, or there might be limitations to the use of the instrument in that particular context that would become apparent only from examining the data over time.

FACTOR INVOLVED

7. Interpretive Feedback

ELEMENTS INVOLVED

71. Willingness to give interpretation and guidance to test takers.
38. Keeping a record of all test data for follow-up, establishing trends, and understanding how the test works in the local situation.

49 DATE MATCHING

SETTING AND APPLICATIONS	Mental Health
INCIDENT	The CompuDate dating service used the 16PF as the sole means of helping clients select their perfect partner. The 16PF was mailed to each client's home, completed, and returned to CompuDate for scoring. Next, 16PF score profiles of possible partners were returned to the client along with the client's own profile. The profile forms were those normally used by professionals to record the standard score profile. No additional interpretive information was provided. Clients matched their profiles with profiles of possible partners and then notified CompuDate of their choice(s).
FOCUS QUESTIONS	What type of interpretive information should be provided to CompuDate clients who have taken the 16PF?
	What type of validity information would you expect to have in order to justify the use of the 16PF in this setting?
	What would CompuDate have to do in order to convince responsible professionals that they are using the 16PF appropriately?

The desire to appear technologically sophisticated in the interest of charging more for services has led to questionable testing practices, some of which are illustrated in this case. However, the use of appropriately validated tests such as the 16PF, properly administered and sensitively interpreted by qualified professionals, might help clarify questions that clients of services such as CompuDate had about themselves and what they were looking for in others. If CompuDate was willing to underwrite this kind of professional service, they should also consider using a more comprehensive assessment procedure.

A profile sheet designed for use by a trained professional is not likely to answer all the questions that the test taker might have. Without additional interpretive material, clients could misinterpret results. The haphazard distribution of psychological test materials and their results might also have the effect of devaluing them in the public mind.

Clients should not receive a test by mail. Instead, clients should complete the questionnaire at the CompuDate office. Neither should test takers receive results through the mail. Instead, a responsible professional at CompuDate should provide feedback to clients. Although the professional might find it useful to show the profile to clients during the feedback session, test profiles themselves should not be left with clients.

2. Proper Test Use
7. Interpretive Feedback
1. Comprehensive Assessment

2. Knowledge of professional ethics.
12. Keeping scoring keys and test materials secure.
16. Using settings for testing that allow for optimum performance by the test takers.
61. Seeing that every examinee follows directions so that test scores are accurate.
72. Ability to give interpretation and guidance to test takers in counseling situations.
60. Establishing rapport with examinees to obtain accurate scores.
78. Referring to a test as a basis for an interpretation only when the test has been properly administered and scored and the interpretation is well validated.
45. Choosing tests sufficient to sample behaviors for a specific purpose.
22. Knowledge of the need for multiple sources of convergent data.

50 THE MISSING PERSONALITY TEST

SETTING AND APPLICATIONS Counseling/Training

INCIDENT Jerry, a high school student who was concerned about choosing a college and about his long-term career goals, sought the help of a counselor. The counselor administered and interpreted the Ball Aptitude Battery and the Strong Interest Inventory. Based on the discussion of his results, Jerry decided to apply to a number of highly competitive engineering schools. He was accepted at one of these schools, which was located in another part of the country.

Six months later Jerry entered therapy with a psychologist because of severe anxiety related to his having to leave home to attend college. With Jerry's permission, the psychologist requested and received the test results from Jerry's former counselor. He used the results of these tests as the basis for a detailed written personality evaluation of the student. This evaluation, which was shared with the student's parents, was to be used as the basis for the treatment and for a recommendation about the best course of action for Jerry.

Jerry's parents, upon reading the report, questioned the accuracy of some of the personality descriptions made by the psychologist. The psychologist stated that he had extensive clinical experience in using aptitude tests and interest inventories in such a manner and that in his expert judgment, the results were quite valid for that purpose. The psychologist had an excellent reputation in the community and had come highly recommended. When pressed further, however, he could not point to specific research that supported the use of these tests in the manner in which he had employed them.

FOCUS QUESTIONS Did Jerry's high school counselor (not the psychologist he saw later) have a professional obligation to evaluate or help Jerry identify any potential anxiety about leaving home in the course of an educational planning session?

What tests could the psychologist have used to evaluate Jerry's anxiety? What interview questions? What other sources of information would be important to explore?

How would a test purporting to measure severe anxiety be validated?

Test scores should be used only for purposes for which they have been validated. The results from aptitude and interest inventories, which are typically administered in career counseling settings, are not likely to contribute much meaningful information for developing a treatment plan for severe anxiety disorders. Harm could result if the misapplied test results led to an inappropriate treatment, or if the parents or student drew erroneous conclusions about the student's personality on the basis of the report.

Every test has certain limitations because of, among other things, the form and content of the particular items to which the client must respond, the extent and quality of the validity research that has been conducted, and how and with whom the test was developed. Such factors place constraints on how scores can be interpreted. A test user must thoroughly understand these limitations before testing and refrain from employing tests that are inappropriate for the particular use, client, or setting.

The psychologist could have determined what personality constructs he desired to measure and then chosen an appropriate personality instrument. For example, there are many instruments specifically designed to measure anxiety and coping that may have been useful in devising a treatment plan for this client. Having identified a number of promising tests, the psychologist should have then examined the documentation provided with the test to determine whether or not evidence existed for the validity of the scores for the purpose for which they were to be used. Even if such validity data existed, it would still be necessary to make a determination as to its applicability to this particular client in this particular situation.

If the psychologist were convinced that his approach was reasonable and valid, he should present his ideas to his colleagues in a professional forum such as a conference or a journal article where his peers could have the opportunity to react and evaluate his approach. Such exposure might eventually lead to the validation of his approach.

FACTORS INVOLVED

1. Comprehensive Assessment
2. Proper Test Use

ELEMENTS INVOLVED

40. Refraining from making evaluations from inappropriate tests.
45. Choosing tests sufficient to sample behaviors for a specific purpose.
47. Avoiding interpretation beyond the limits of the test.
17. Knowledge of the test and its limitations.

51 TEST RESULTS WITHOUT INTERPRETATION

SETTING AND APPLICATIONS

Mental Health

INCIDENT

A student was referred to a speech and language clinic because of suspected language processing problems. The parent stated on the application form that the student had been evaluated by a psychologist 3 months earlier. With parental consent, the speech-language pathologist requested a copy of the psychologist's report. Instead, the psychologist sent a copy of the Wechsler Intelligence Scale for Children–Revised (WISC-R) record form he had completed in his evaluation, with no accompanying report or interpretation of the test results.

FOCUS QUESTION

What elements might one expect to be included in a report primarily involving the interpretation of WISC-R results?

The psychologist should not have sent only a copy of the WISC-R record form, which, predictably, was not helpful to the speech-language pathologist. The psychologist should have sent a copy of his report. Interpretation of test performance requires the integration of test data with background information, behavioral observations made during testing, and possibly other factors, all of which should have been components of the psychologist's written report of the assessment. The psychologist's failure to send the report could have resulted in someone's attempting to interpret the results on the record form alone.

FACTOR INVOLVED

2. Proper Test Use

ELEMENTS INVOLVED

2. Knowledge of professional ethics.
75. Interpreting test scores to parents and teachers, rather than simply transmitting scores labeling the child without considering compensating strengths and actual school performance.

52 CONFUSING NORM-REFERENCED AND CRITERION-REFERENCED TESTS

SETTING AND
APPLICATIONS
Education

INCIDENT
For several years, a medium-sized southern school district had administered to all grade 4 pupils a criterion-referenced mathematics test prepared by the state department of education based on the state mathematics curriculum guidelines. The test was optional and was used by local school districts to gauge the extent to which district pupils met the established criterion of 80% of items correct on the various content areas measured by the test. The district decided to discontinue the test when the California Achievement Test (CAT) was adopted in grades 4–8 to meet the need for norm-referenced test information. In fact, school officials believed that the CAT results would provide the same type of information as the state-developed criterion-referenced test and, in addition, would provide national normative data.

After administration of the CAT and scoring by the publisher's scoring service, a fourth-grade teacher received her class list report of scores and noticed that check marks appeared beside the names of about three fourths of her pupils. An administrative memorandum accompanying the class list directed the teacher to begin planning remedial instruction in mathematics for those pupils whose names were checked. The teacher was especially puzzled because she noted a number of students checked whose performance in mathematics was quite good compared with both her present and past students. Upon inquiring about the students whose names were marked, she was told that the school district central office staff had marked the names of all students whose total mathematics percentile rank was below 80. This was done for every class in the district because the criterion of mastery required on the previous state-developed test was 80 percent of items correct. This teacher, who had just completed a course in tests and measurements, immediately saw the error her administrative staff had made, and she began to consider just what action she should take next.

FOCUS
QUESTIONS
What error did the administrative staff make?

What course of action should the teacher take? What should the administrative staff do? How can the district get the type of information needed in order to identify students in need of remediation?

In what way does percentage of items correct differ from the percentile rank of a certain score?

The local school officials made two obvious errors. First, they failed to realize the basic differences between the state-developed criterion-referenced test to assess mastery of the recommended fourth-grade state curriculum and a nationally developed norm-referenced survey test designed to assess skills common to diverse school districts throughout the nation and to differentiate among pupils on the various skill domains measured by the test. A subsequent comparison of the content of the tests showed marked differences and underscored the fact that the two tests were designed for quite different uses and that the norm-referenced mathematics test could not be substituted for the criterion-referenced state test.

A second misuse occurred when pupils having a total mathematics percentile rank below 80 were marked for remediation follow-up. Administrators confused 80% of items correct, the mastery criterion on the state test, with a percentile rank of 80. The two scores are quite different. A percentile rank of 80 means that a student's raw score in mathematics equaled or exceeded that of 80 percent of pupils in the national norm group, whereas 80% correct merely makes a statement about how a student performed in relation to the total number of items on the test. In addition, users cannot automatically apply cut scores set on one test (e.g., 80% of items correct) to another test without establishing the equivalence of both test content and test items.

Serious repercussions could result from the misidentification of students for remediation when many of these students were not in need of such efforts. Many parents would likely become outraged at having their children incorrectly classified for remedial work, especially if it became known that this resulted from an administrative error. A great deal of time and effort would be wasted, not to mention the negative publicity and embarrassment to the administrative staff that would be incurred.

In order to rectify this situation, the district administrative staff should direct the teachers to ignore the marks beside the names of students on their class lists. Although the CAT does not provide the same type of information as the previous criterion-referenced test, teachers should be shown how to use the results reported on specific CAT skill clusters, because this information can suggest possible areas for further exploration in gaining an understanding of individual strengths and weaknesses.

FACTORS INVOLVED

2. Proper Test Use
4. Maintaining Integrity of Test Results
3. Psychometric Knowledge

ELEMENTS INVOLVED

17. Knowledge of the test and its limitations.
34. Considering whether the reason for giving a test locally meets the purpose for which the test was designed.
41. Understanding standard scores and percentile ranks.

53 PSYCHOLOGICAL TESTS FOR CHILDREN WITH HEARING IMPAIRMENTS

SETTING AND APPLICATIONS

Speech-Language-Hearing

INCIDENT

A 5-year-old child with a moderate hearing loss was tested for educational placement by a school district diagnostician. On the basis of psychological test results obtained from a standard test battery, the child was recommended for placement in a Total Communication Classroom for children with hearing impairments, that is, a classroom in which a combination of auditory training, speechreading, and sign language is used. The placement decision was based on the moderate hearing loss shown by pure tone audiometric screening results and the "marked language delay" revealed by language testing. The parents refused this placement, believing that the child was capable of functioning in a regular classroom, that is, a mainstream placement. On the advice of consultants, the parents pointed out that two errors in the evaluation had been made. First, complete tests of the child's auditory perceptual abilities had not been carried out, and, second, the language and intelligence tests used had not been standardized on children with hearing impairments and therefore penalized this child. In subsequent testing carried out by a private testing group, full audiological testing showed that the child was capable of functioning with hearing aids in a regular classroom. Results of language tests normed on children with hearing impairments suggested that the child had a good prognosis for development of auditory and speech skills.

FOCUS QUESTIONS

When is it appropriate to compare test results of an individual with a hearing impairment with a group with normal hearing and with a group with hearing impairment?

What are the differences between the concepts of standardization of tests and norming of tests?

A more appropriate recommendation for the placement of this child would have been made had the appropriate consultation and referral to an audiologist and speech-language pathologist been made. The audiologist would have provided complete audiological testing and the speech-language pathologist would have assessed the child's speech and language abilities. Using a team approach in consultation with the school district diagnostician and the child's teacher, the team could have obtained a more complete and accurate picture of the child's functioning and prognosis for his ability to succeed in a regular classroom.

The general educational community is often unaware (a) that the population with hearing impairment is substantially different from that with normal hearing when auditory/verbal experience is considered and (b) that tests normed on subjects with normal hearing necessarily penalize persons with hearing impairments. In this case, the state standards did not require the use of appropriately standardized tests for use with a child with a hearing loss. The school diagnostician was unaware that special tests should have been used with this child and that using conventionally normed tests was discriminatory. The conventionally normed instruments simply reflected the child's language difficulties due to his hearing loss rather than his intelligence.

State and local educational authorities need to recognize that when children with disabilities, such as hearing impairment, are evaluated, the use of norms derived from children without such disabilities may be inappropriate and may result in inaccurate descriptions of a client's abilities. Diagnosticians, too, need to be conscious to select tests that are appropriate for the test taker and to keep up with the literature on special assessment needs of specific subgroups.

For the child in this case, the parents were interested in an educational placement that offered an oral/auditory approach to speech and language development. A diagnostic profile of this child using appropriate measurement instruments for persons with hearing impairment indicated that the child had the necessary cognitive and auditory capabilities for functioning in a mainstreamed environment.

FACTOR INVOLVED

1. Comprehensive Assessment

ELEMENTS INVOLVED

67. Selecting tests appropriate to both the purpose of measurement and to the test takers.
35. Recognizing, in a clinical setting, when a patient's state has been misdiagnosed or has changed, and selecting suitable norms.
28. Keeping up with the field and checking one's own interpretations with others.
83. Being concerned with the individual differences of test takers rather than presenting test scores directly from descriptions in the manual or computer printout.

54 THE GHASTLY GIFTED CUT-OFF SCORE

SETTING AND APPLICATIONS

Education

INCIDENT

To identify students for its program for the gifted, a school district used the Otis-Lennon School Ability Test and supplemented the Otis-Lennon with the California Achievement Test (CAT) and a locally developed Likert rating scale that was completed by a student's regular classroom teacher. The rating scale had been developed by a team of teachers in the gifted program, although no data had been collected to support its psychometric qualities; the rating scale included teacher's perceptions of such things as student motivation, work habits, and special interests and talents. The use of three different measures was intended to provide information on several dimensions of the student's abilities.

To be considered for the gifted program, a student was required to have a School Ability Index of at least 130 (reported on a standard score scale with a mean of 100 and standard deviation of 15) on the Otis-Lennon. Below that level, a student was not considered regardless of scores on the CAT or ratings by his or her teacher. If students achieved the minimum School Ability Index of 130, they would be selected for the gifted program if they had a CAT total battery percentile rank of 90 or higher and teacher ratings that were "generally positive."

FOCUS QUESTIONS

What are the advantages of the school district's selection criteria for the gifted program?
What are the problems with the selection criteria?
What are potential negative consequences of using the school district's selection criteria?
What would be more appropriate selection criteria? How would these be better than the school district's current criteria?

Staff members of the aforementioned school district were aware of the desirability of using information from several sources in identifying gifted students. For that reason, they decided to use achievement test scores and teacher ratings to supplement scholastic ability scores, although the students must have achieved the minimum cut-off score on the aptitude test. The staff members' decisions were based on the following criteria: (a) The School Ability Index cut-off point was set at a level that could be defended as "gifted"; and (b) the use of an absolute cut-off reduced the likelihood of arguments from unsophisticated parents whose children's Otis-Lennon scores fell just short of 130.

The identification procedures used by the school district could result in improperly identified students. The most serious result would be for those students who fell below the School Ability Index cut-off score. They might be as well qualified as some students who were selected, but because of the selection procedures would be denied entrance to the program for gifted students. Problems with the school district's identification procedures included the following: (a) use of an absolute cut-off score on the Otis-Lennon before a student would even be considered for the gifted program; (b) failure to recognize and account for the standard error of measurement in the norm-referenced Otis-Lennon and the CAT; (c) use of a locally developed rating scale with undetermined reliability and validity; (d) use of only three measures in the selection criteria, with two of the three focusing on academic abilities, resulting in de-emphasis on other important skills and aptitudes of students; and (e) over-reliance on students' performance on standardized, norm-referenced tests, which may be affected by test-taking skills, anxiety, and other factors, and may not always give the best prediction of students' potential success in the gifted program.

Revisions that could be adopted (and in fact later were) by the school district to rectify problems in the identification procedures include the following:

1. Orienting school district personnel involved in the identification process to (a) psychometric characteristics of norm-referenced, standardized tests, particularly the concepts of standard error of measurement, reliability, and validity, with specific applications to the Otis-Lennon and the CAT; (b) alternative sources of information that would be useful in determining which students could benefit most from special programs; and (c) the need to determine reliability and validity of all these data as selection criteria for programs for the gifted.

2. Orienting all district administrative and teaching staff to the limitations and strengths of standardized tests and nonstandardized assessments, such as their locally developed rating scale.

3. Rather than using an absolute cut-off point, taking the limitations of tests into account by using the following criteria for gifted program selection: (a) students with School Ability Indexes at and above 130 would be accepted for the gifted program; and (b) students with School Ability Indexes below 130 would receive further consideration, including examination of scores on the CAT, teachers' ratings, and additional evidence provided by students, teachers, counselors, and parents—such as performance and work samples, assessments of creativity and higher level reasoning skills, and assessments of skills and aptitudes that go beyond scholastic aptitude and achievement.

1. Comprehensive Assessment
2. Proper Test Use
3. Psychometric Knowledge
4. Maintaining Integrity of Test Results

8. Providing appropriate training and quality control over operations for all users of tests and test results.
22. Knowledge of the need for multiple sources of convergent data.
32. Considering the standard error of measurement.
49. Making clear that absolute cut-off scores imposed for placement in special programs for the gifted are questionable because they ignore measurement error.

55 DEVELOPING A SELECTION BATTERY

SETTING AND APPLICATIONS

Employment

INCIDENT

A large manufacturer asked a consultant to develop a selection battery for jobs that required relatively low skill levels in one of its plants. Management's goal was to select employees who were average or below average in intelligence. The presumption was that by matching the demands of the job to the ability level of the employees, the company would have less turnover. A battery consisting of three cognitive ability tests was recommended by the consultant and utilized by the firm's personnel department. The battery was administered to applicants with the standard instructions.

FOCUS QUESTIONS

What other factors might be considered in selecting people for jobs that do not have high cognitive demands?

What consequences might a company experience as a result of using an unvalidated selection battery?

Does it seem reasonable to reject overqualified applicants?

The consultant proceeded without questioning an assumption that the selection of average or below-average workers would lead to less turnover. Even though this belief may have been widely held throughout the company and may even have seemed reasonable to the consultant, it must be verified.

The major issue in this case is the lack of validation. Without data, it is almost certain that potentially qualified applicants would be rejected. At a minimum, the consultant should have conducted a study to examine the relationship between scores on the selection examination and quitting. In addition, the consultant might have examined other factors (e.g., job design, supervisory practices, and compensation) that contributed more to turnover than high intelligence.

There are additional issues related to this strategy as a selection technique. In this situation, the successful applicant is one who does poorly on the examinations. However, the instructions for most cognitive ability tests advise examinees to do their best. Is it fair to ask applicants to do their best when doing so means that they will probably be rejected?

When the situation arises, consultants must explain to organizations why a request is unethical, unjustified, or otherwise inappropriate. Upon reflection, such requests are usually not in the company's best interests. In this case, the absence of validation data to support such an unusual application of test results could put the company at risk of a lawsuit. The consultant should have explained the necessity of doing a careful study of the matter before uncritically implementing a testing program. Consultants must struggle with ethically ambiguous issues and attempt to resolve conflicts among ethical and technical standards that will minimize the potential harm to all parties.

FACTORS INVOLVED

1. Comprehensive Assessment
3. Psychometric Knowledge
2. Proper Test Use

ELEMENTS INVOLVED

27. Appreciating the implications of test validity.
3. Maintaining proper actions regardless of management pressures.
5. Knowledge of legal standards.
24. Recognizing that although test scores are observed, knowledges, skills, abilities, and personal characteristics may be observed in performance but are only inferred from test scores.
40. Refraining from making evaluations from inappropriate tests.

56 INAPPROPRIATE INTERPRETATION OF THE SECONDARY SCHOOL ADMISSION TEST

SETTING AND APPLICATIONS

Education

INCIDENT

The admissions director at an independent secondary school reported to the test publisher that he could determine the sexual orientation of male applicants to his school by their Secondary School Admission Test (SSAT) verbal and math scores: Higher math than verbal scores meant that the boy was heterosexual and higher verbal than math scores meant that the boy was homosexual. The admissions director indicated that his experience with several students had led him to this conclusion. No amount of remonstration and no appeal to reason or attention to other evidence would change his mind.

FOCUS QUESTIONS

What harm could result from the admission director's contention?

Does the test publisher have an obligation to take any action about the admission director's contention?

If the admissions director communicated his contention to students, parents, and school personnel, or used his contention in admissions decisions, should he be reported for unethical conduct? If he did not communicate or use his contention, should he be reported?

An interpretation that uses SSAT scores to determine sexual orientation is totally lacking in scientific basis and raises serious questions about the competency of the admissions director. It is not known whether the admissions director had actually communicated this interpretation to parents, students, and school personnel or whether admissions decisions had been made on the basis of this interpretation. To do so would represent a serious abrogation of ethical principles, not to mention possible discrimination based on perceived sexual orientation. The admissions director should again be informed of the lack of any reliable evidence to support his interpretation and the potential consequences that any actions based on this interpretation could have in damaging the students as well as the reputations of the school and the test. If the test publisher determined that the admissions director was communicating this interpretation or making admissions decisions based on this interpretation, then the test publisher should explore the option of reporting the admissions director for unethical conduct.

FACTORS INVOLVED

1. Comprehensive Assessment
2. Proper Test Use
3. Psychometric Knowledge

ELEMENTS INVOLVED

1. Accepting responsibility for competent use of the test.
2. Knowledge of professional ethics.
17. Knowledge of the test and its limitations.
27. Appreciating the implications of test validity.
40. Refraining from making evaluations from inappropriate tests.
47. Avoiding interpretation beyond the limits of the test.

57 IMMIGRANTS LOSE FINANCIALLY

SETTING AND
APPLICATIONS

Mental Health

INCIDENT

Plaintiffs (all Hispanic) in a lawsuit alleged that they had, in good faith, deposited money with an organization that claimed to provide banking services not otherwise available to undocumented individuals residing in the United States. They claimed that the business then ceased operations and refused to refund their money. In addition to recovery of their funds, the plaintiffs sought compensation for emotional distress. A mental health professional was hired by the plaintiffs' attorneys to determine if the plaintiffs were suffering from emotional distress and stress-related disorders owing to financial loss and fraud.

The mental health professional administered a "short form" of the Minnesota Multiphasic Personality Inventory (MMPI), the MMPI-168, to all 158 plaintiffs. The test was administered in Spanish. The mental health professional, who had no training or expertise in testing, chose the MMPI-168 without consulting a professional with expertise in MMPI assessment or a consultant with expertise in mental health issues specific to the Hispanic community. He offered the following reasons for his choice of the MMPI-168: (a) The MMPI is a "proven diagnostic instrument" with high credibility in the courtroom; (b) the MMPI is appropriate to the evaluation of multicultural populations; (c) the MMPI is sensitive to stress-related disorders; (d) the Spanish version of the MMPI is reliable and valid for the assessment of individuals such as the plaintiffs; (e) the MMPI-168 is just as valid as the standard MMPI; and (f) the MMPI can be used in epidemiological fashion to determine the prevalence of psychiatric disorders in a specified population.

About 2 years after the plaintiffs initially filed their suit, the MMPI-168 was administered to all the plaintiffs in a group setting. Spanish-speaking paraprofessionals served as "interpreters" and "translators" for some of the plaintiffs who were able to complete the MMPI-168 only with such assistance. The plaintiffs were instructed to report any mental health problems that could be used to aid their cause. The mental health professional performed no other assessment of the plaintiffs.

Information gathered during the lawsuit indicated that the plaintiffs were under stresses unrelated to their cause of action. Many had fled oppressive countries. Being undocumented, many were afraid of deportation. Indeed, some were or had been involved in deportation proceedings. As a result, they were very careful about disclosing personal information. Some were experiencing other stressful events, such as a death in the family.

The mental health professional testified, in a pretrial deposition, that the MMPI-168 results confirmed that the plaintiffs were suffering from nonpsychotic stress disorders owing to financial loss.

FOCUS
QUESTIONS

What procedures could have been used by the mental health professional to determine whether the plaintiffs were suffering from stress owing to their dealings with the banking services organization?

How might administering the MMPI-168 in a group situation have affected the plaintiffs' test results?

Many of the mental health professional's actions in selecting and using the MMPI-168 were inappropriate. He selected the MMPI largely because of its reputation, apparently without careful consideration of the appropriateness of its use with the plaintiffs. He considered no possible alternatives to the MMPI, nor did he use other assessment techniques. He did not consider conventional rules for determining MMPI profile validity. He did not consider the potential for data contamination owing to plaintiff test-taking attitudes, much less the probable impact of the nonstandard instructions given the plaintiffs when they completed the MMPI-168. He did not consider the implications of limitations in reading ability among the plaintiffs, who had an average of 3 years of education. Nor did he consider the possible impact of his unprecedented use of "translators" and "interpreters" to help the plaintiffs complete the MMPI-168.

An evaluation of the mental health professional's use of the MMPI-168 by an expert in Hispanic MMPI research revealed the following: (a) The majority of the plaintiffs' MMPI-168 results were of questionable validity, owing to extremely high scores on the instrument's validity scales; (b) the clinical scale scores often appeared to be highly exaggerated, further calling into question the validity of the results; (c) the MMPI-168 results, interpreted collectively and without considering other information, were consistent with a psychotic degree of emotional distress; (d) the MMPI-168 alone cannot document the presence of any psychiatric disorder; (e) use of an MMPI-168 administered 2 years after an alleged trauma to document a stress disorder caused by that trauma is questionable at best; (f) use of the MMPI norms based on White Americans to interpret the protocols of ethnic/racial minorities is a source of continuing controversy among MMPI scholars; (g) the mental health professional did not review the literature on Hispanic MMPI performance; (h) no other potential moderator variables (e.g., acculturation, intelligence, or socioeconomic status) were considered in the interpretation of the MMPI-168 results; and (i) the validity of the MMPI-168 as a substitute for the full MMPI is a source of continuing controversy among MMPI scholars.

The neutral expert concluded that the mental health professional's incomplete examination of the plaintiffs and his improper use of the MMPI-168 would probably have had a severe adverse effect on the plaintiffs' case if it had ever come to trial. Presumably, the defendant's attorney would have exposed the flaws in the mental health professional's evaluation upon cross-examination. The case was settled out of court.

FACTORS INVOLVED

1. Comprehensive Assessment
2. Proper Test Use
3. Psychometric Knowledge
4. Maintaining Integrity of Test Results

ELEMENTS INVOLVED

2. Knowledge of professional ethics.
7. Refraining from helping a favored person get a good score.
13. Refraining from modifying prescribed administration procedures to adapt to particular individuals.
17. Knowledge of the test and its limitations.
18. Perceiving the score on a test as representing only one period of time, subject to change from experience.
22. Knowledge of the need for multiple sources of convergent data.
25. Understanding norms and their limitations.
27. Appreciating the implications of test validity.
28. Keeping up with the field and checking one's own interpretations with others.
35. Recognizing, in a clinical setting, when a patient's state has been misdiagnosed or has changed, and selecting suitable norms.
52. Understanding statistical data in the pattern of evaluation.
54. Based on valid information, taking account of those elements in a test that discriminate against certain populations.
67. Selecting tests appropriate to both the purpose of measurement and to the test takers.

68. Selecting tests that are as free from discrimination as possible, considering the standardization sample and the test-taker population.

34. Considering whether the reason for giving the test locally meets the purpose for which the test was designed.

23. Skill in taking a good history to integrate with test results.

58 INCONSISTENCIES BETWEEN TEST RESULTS AND BEHAVIOR

SETTING AND APPLICATIONS

Neuropsychology

INCIDENT

A 45-year-old woman was referred to a medical center for evaluation after being in a motor vehicle accident that resulted in 2 minutes of loss of consciousness, a feeling of being "dazed," and headache. She had no skull fractures and was released after spending several hours in an emergency room. She was evaluated by a neuropsychologist 2 years later in conjunction with a lawsuit in which she claimed to have continuing cognitive deficits that were secondary to the head injury sustained in the accident. A brain scan was conducted and the results were negative.

The neuropsychologist conducted an assessment of brain functioning, administering a variety of tests that assessed the woman's psychometric intelligence, memory, and attention. He also administered the Minnesota Multiphasic Personality Inventory (MMPI) and found the results to be within normal limits. The neuropsychologist found that the patient's performance on all of the other tests administered showed severe impairment. He interpreted these findings to be indicative of residuals of the reported closed head injury, allowing her to gain disability compensation. The valid MMPI was used as confirmation that malingering or depression could not explain the test taker's behavior. This conclusion was drawn despite inconsistencies between the test taker's behavior during interview and the test scores. For example, the patient was able to answer all questions on interview without difficulty, but formal assessment of her auditory comprehension revealed severe comprehension deficits. In addition, the fact that she could concentrate and read well enough to produce a valid MMPI is inconsistent with severe cognitive deficits.

FOCUS QUESTION

What explanation can you offer for the neuropsychologist's apparent failure to ignore his nontest data?

The assessor did not integrate the patient's history with her test findings. If there were a head injury, it would be judged mild by all criteria. Such an injury could certainly produce subtle cognitive deficits, but those deficits would usually be recovered 2 years after injury. At any rate, the degree of deficit demonstrated by this patient would be extremely unlikely after an injury of the severity claimed.

The assessor should have considered other possible explanations, including malingering for possible secondary gain. This is certainly possible even with a normal-limits MMPI if the patient is focusing upon physical rather than psychological symptoms.

1. Comprehensive Assessment
2. Proper Test Use

23. Skill in taking a good history to integrate with test results.
10. Being alert to test takers who show passive or aggressive nonparticipation.
17. Knowledge of the test and its limitations.

59 CONSIDERING LESS THAN HALF THE PROBLEM

SETTING AND
APPLICATIONS
Neuropsychology

INCIDENT

A right-handed patient had suffered a stroke on the left side of the brain 2 years before he was referred to a neuropsychologist to determine whether he had deficits consistent with another stroke. The assessor administered a large number of tests, including tests of language and spatial skills, attention and concentration, memory and learning, flexible problem solving, simultaneous processing, rapid information processing, and response inhibition, alternation, and sequencing. Based upon the finding that the patient could not draw even simple geometric forms, such as squares, circles, or diamonds, the assessor concluded the patient had spatial deficits consistent with a stroke in the right half of the brain. Mild problems in phonemic discrimination (nine errors on the Speech-Sounds Perception Test) and word pronunciation (one error on the Halstead Indiana Aphasia Examination) were interpreted as indicating mild residuals of the first stroke. As documented in the analysis, it turned out that the patient's difficulties had other causes.

FOCUS QUESTION

What harm to the patient might result from the misdiagnosis of a stroke?

The examiner did not take a complete history. As a result, he did not know the patient had a mild paralysis of the right side of his body as a result of the first stroke and a recent severe arm/hand injury. These problems were sufficient to preclude the fine motor control required for drawing.

The examiner should have administered tests of spatial functioning that are less dependent upon motor skills (e.g., Facial Recognition, Judgment of Line Orientation, or Hooper Test of Visual Organization) to determine if spatial difficulties alone could account for the problem. The assessor also did not administer simple motor tasks (e.g., finger tapping, or grip strength) to determine if motor deficits alone could account for the problem. Finally, testing motor skills in the left arm would have provided another piece of evidence very useful in detecting the presence or absence of a stroke in the right hemisphere.

FACTOR INVOLVED

1. Comprehensive Assessment

ELEMENTS INVOLVED

45. Choosing tests sufficient to sample behaviors for a specific purpose.
23. Skill in taking a good history to integrate with test results.

60 APPROPRIATE USE OF A GRADE EQUIVALENT SCORE FOR A STUDENT WITH A HEARING IMPAIRMENT

SETTING AND APPLICATIONS   Education

INCIDENT   Because of its good match to the school's curriculum and because of the availability of special norms for children with hearing impairments, Ms. Johnson used the Stanford Achievement Test in the April testing of her third-grade class. She used special administration procedures for her mainstreamed student with a hearing impairment.

Although most of the students in Ms. Johnson's class were assigned the Primary 3 level of the Stanford based on their grade in school (this level measures achievement in curriculum content typically taught in grades 3.5 to 4.5), Ms. Johnson realized that she must determine which level(s) of the test would be most appropriate for Jenny, a 10-year-old girl with a hearing impairment who was integrated with her regular classmates for instruction in all subjects except reading and language arts. Age- or grade-based test level assignments are not necessarily appropriate for children with hearing impairments, who often progress at different rates in various school subjects.

Ms. Johnson examined the instructional objectives booklet in reading comprehension and mathematics computation provided by the Center for Assessment and Demographic Studies (CADS). She thereby determined which level of these two subtests matched up best with Jenny's curriculum and instruction. The Primary 2 level appeared to be appropriate for the reading-related subtests, and Primary 3 appeared to be appropriate for mathematics. In class, Jenny had shown facility with the kinds of whole number arithmetical operations that comprised 82% of the Primary 3 mathematics computation subtest, and she had recently been exposed to the remaining content (18%). The Primary 3 level appeared to be an appropriate level to allow Jenny to answer between 40% and 80% of the items correctly, the recommended target range for the most precise measurement.

Following the CADS recommendations for using the Stanford with test takers with hearing impairments, Ms. Johnson then administered the Primary 2 reading comprehension and Primary 3 mathematics computation screening tests to Jenny. These short screening tests allowed Jenny to practice the kinds of items she would encounter in the actual subtests.

At testing time, Jenny was administered the Stanford mathematics computation subtest, along with her classmates. Jenny took the Primary 2 reading comprehension and other reading-related subtests separately from her classmates. All these tests were administered with the directions and sample items communicated in sign language, the same mode of communication used during daily instruction, and the standard time limits were followed.

Jenny's score report showed that she answered 38 of the 44 (86%) mathematics computation subtest items correctly, corresponding to a scaled score of 648 and a grade equivalent of 6.1 (extrapolated from the test normed at 3.5 to 4.5). Using the norms for children with hearing impairments developed by CADS in 1990, Jenny's scaled score was at the 92nd percentile when compared with scores for all 10-year olds with hearing impairments. Using the standard norms provided by the publisher, Jenny's scaled score was at the 87th percentile of the Spring Grade 3 norm group.

Jenny's Stanford score report was examined at the Individual Educational Planning (IEP) meeting to plan her education for the next year. Because of Jenny's high grade equivalent (6.1) in mathematics computation, Jenny's parents requested that Jenny be placed in a sixth-grade mathematics class in the fall, because "she is obviously doing sixth-grade work in mathematics." Ms. Johnson agreed, noting Jenny's scores in normed groups.

FOCUS QUESTIONS   Was Jenny doing sixth-grade work in mathematics?
Would it be advisable to put Jenny in a sixth-grade mathematics class in the fall?
How could the test scores have been explained to the parents in a manner that would have changed their request to a more appropriate one for Jenny?

The selection of the Stanford Achievement Test was correctly based upon its match to the students' curriculum and the availability of appropriate norms for the students with normal and with impaired hearing in the class. The Primary 3 level of the test measures curriculum content typically taught students nationally in grades 3.5 to 4.5, making this level appropriate for many students in the spring semester of third grade. The selection of reading and mathematics subtest levels for the students with hearing impairments was done correctly. Also, Ms. Johnson was correct in selecting test levels that would allow Jenny's score to be in the middle of the score range where the standard error of measurement is smaller, for measurement error increases when scores approach the chance level of the scores on the test. Test administration for Jenny also was conducted correctly, with adherence to the usual time limits and with test directions given using the mode of communication commonly used in Jenny's classroom.

Test score interpretation, however, was not altogether correct. One could assume that Jenny's mathematics score of 38 (86%) correct was valid, for the test measured content related closely to her classroom instruction and Jenny was familiar with the testing format. It was appropriate to compare Jenny's performance with a norm group of students her age with hearing impairments, for she had a hearing impairment. It was also appropriate and meaningful to examine Jenny's scores in light of the national Grade 3 Spring norms, for Jenny was integrated with hearing students in a regular classroom for mathematics instruction. However, it was not appropriate to claim that Jenny was "doing sixth-grade math." Jenny was performing very well on a test that measures performance in third- and fourth-grade mathematics—as well as a new sixth-grader might be expected to perform on this test. But the test content is clearly not sixth-grade.

Ms. Johnson failed to consult other professionals experienced in interpreting test scores and to adhere to professional standards in test interpretation in several respects. She failed to appreciate the content coverage of the test. She failed to understand the norms and their limitations when she neglected to explain the grade equivalent score in light of the content level of the test. She further failed to consider multiple sources of convergent data in agreeing to recommend that Jenny be placed in a sixth-grade mathematics class in the fall, based on her performance on only one test. Finally, she failed to accept the responsibility for the competent use of the test by allowing the student's parents to suggest an inappropriate action and agreeing with that action.

FACTORS INVOLVED

1. Comprehensive Assessment
2. Proper Test Use
3. Psychometric Knowledge
7. Interpretive Feedback

ELEMENTS INVOLVED

26. Appreciating the limitations of content coverage.
25. Understanding norms and their limitations.
22. Knowledge of the need for multiple sources of convergent data.
1. Accepting responsibility for competent use of the test.
67. Selecting tests appropriate to both the purpose of measurement and to the test takers.
46. Interpreting test results properly for the particular group tested, keeping in mind the characteristics of that group.
29. Applying principles of test theory and principles of test interpretation.
20. Considering errors of measurement of a test score.
44. Understanding standard errors of estimate and standard errors of measurement.

61 Narrowing Options

Setting and Applications

Education

Incident

A school guidance counselor received the results of the April testing of all 11th-grade students in his school on the Armed Services Vocational Aptitude Battery (ASVAB). Information provided to the counselor on each student included composite scores in general learning ability and verbal and math ability, in addition to scores on 10 separate tests in the battery. Scores for each test and composite were provided as percentiles and percentile bands, representing comparisons to a nationally representative sample of students.

The school counselor made it a practice to spend time with each student during individual counseling sessions to review the test results and to suggest courses in which they might enroll in grade 12. Job possibilities and future education for the student were also discussed.

In a test interpretation session with Vanessa, the counselor reviewed her general learning ability and her verbal and math scores compared to students of her same and opposite sex. Her scores were at about the 85th percentile when compared to both groups. This was substantiated by a grade-point average in the B− to B+ range. Her other test results, especially those for mechanical comprehension, electronics information, and auto and shop were lower. When compared to males of her same grade, Vanessa scored at about the 50th percentile in these subtests and, when compared to females, her percentile scores were at about the 66th percentile. Her speeded tests were fairly high, at about the 80th percentile when compared to her own sex, and at the 87th percentile when compared to 11th-grade males. The speeded subtests show that she seemed able to work fast and to attend to detail.

When speaking to the counselor, Vanessa expressed a tentative desire to enter the field of electronics because she was interested in understanding how things work and in fixing them when they are broken. She told the counselor that she had not taken any related school courses at her high school but thought that she had a knack for fixing things and had just started to spend some Saturdays helping her father at his radio and repair shop. She had also thought about taking basic electronics as an elective course the following year to see whether or not she really liked this kind of work. Because her family did not have the resources to send her to college, she was not planning on obtaining education beyond high school, except perhaps for some specialized training courses at the local community college.

The counselor suggested that, although she performed well on most of the ASVAB tests, she did not perform as well on the technical subtests. He suggested that her scores on the speeded tests indicated that she might consider being an accountant or a secretary because she seemed able to work fast and accurately. The counselor proposed to Vanessa that she think about enrolling in a word processing class and a bookkeeping course offered in the first semester of her senior year. Vanessa left the counseling session confused over her future and unclear about what courses she would enroll in the following year.

Focus Questions

How should the counselor have used the gender-based norms provided by the ASVAB?
What suggestions should the counselor have made to Vanessa?
How should the counselor have used the information about the percentile bands?

The counselor focused on some of Vanessa's scores but ignored others of importance. It would have been helpful to attend to Vanessa's relatively high score on the general ability composite, which indicated that her ability to learn new material is quite good. Both her test results and her grade point average attest to this fact. She thus seems to have the potential to perform quite well in academic or training courses. Given the interpretive bands provided with the ASVAB, Vanessa's true percentile score could lie between about the 81st and the 89th percentiles. The counselor focused only on the percentile point and did not take into account the information conveyed by the percentile band.

Although her scores on the technical tests were about average compared to males, they were better when compared with females. Vanessa had, without benefit of formal courses, been able to pick up skills and abilities that allowed her to perform better than most females of her age group. Given formal training, she would be likely to improve her knowledge substantially in the technical areas.

The counselor narrowed Vanessa's options to the clerical occupations merely because she performed well on the tests requiring speed and accuracy, skills and abilities that are valuable in many occupations. This fact, along with Vanessa's strong expressed interests in other occupational areas, suggests that the counselor erred by focusing her options too narrowly. She had demonstrated not only an interest but also the ability to at least try out some of the courses that she had proposed.

The counselor could also have explored with Vanessa a variety of ways that she might obtain education and training beyond high school with minimal financial burden to herself or her family such as work-study programs, military training, scholarships, and apprenticeships.

FACTORS INVOLVED

1. Comprehensive Assessment
3. Psychometric Knowledge
7. Interpretive Feedback

ELEMENTS INVOLVED

18. Perceiving the score on a test as representing only one period in time, subject to change from experience.
22. Knowledge of the need for multiple sources of convergent data.
20. Considering errors of measurement of a test score.
32. Considering the standard error of measurement.
44. Understanding standard errors of estimate and standard errors of measurement.
46. Interpreting test results properly for the particular group tested, keeping in mind the characteristics of that group.

Section 7

Reporting to Clients

62 BORDERLINE PRACTICE

SETTING AND
APPLICATIONS
Mental Health

INCIDENT

A psychologist required all of his adult clients to take the Minnesota Multiphasic Personality Inventory (MMPI). The booklet form of the MMPI and a separate answer sheet were given to them at the close of the first session. Clients were told how to mark their answers. They completed the MMPI at home. Then they mailed the booklet and answer sheet back to the psychologist or returned them at their next appointment. The psychologist sent the answer sheets to a test scoring service from which he received a score profile and computer-generated narrative interpretation.

The psychologist did not usually report results to the client. If the client asked specifically about the MMPI, the psychologist would show the profile and offer interpretive comments. These brief interpretations were based on individual scale elevations. In addition, the psychologist referred to each scale by its original clinical designation, for example, "depression," "psychopathic deviate," and "schizophrenia." If the client requested a copy of the profile, the psychologist provided it.

In a few instances, clients requested in writing that the MMPI results be sent to another professional. The psychologist forwarded a copy of the profile, without the narrative interpretation, and then charged the client the full fee for the original reporting service.

FOCUS
QUESTIONS

Does the psychologist have an obligation to report the results back to each of the clients who took the MMPI?

Would developing a computer-generated narrative interpretation using only terms comprehensible to laypersons be sufficient to help the clients interpret their MMPI results?

Should a test publisher be obliged to discontinue elements of tests regarded by experts as obsolete (in this case, labeling MMPI scales "depression," "schizophrenia," etc.)?

Most questionnaires are untimed and fairly self-explanatory. This has led many test users to believe that control of the test administration process itself is unimportant. However, administration of a sensitive, intrusive test like the MMPI should be supervised.

The interpretation of test results in terms of technical diagnostic terminology is likely only to confuse laypeople. They may not realize that elevations on Scale 8 are not of themselves sufficient to diagnose schizophrenia. Furthermore, artificially simplified test interpretation procedures will lead to inadequate interpretations. In this case, the psychologist's scale-by-scale interpretation left it up to clients to synthesize the MMPI results. It was the psychologist's responsibility to synthesize the MMPI results and integrate them with other information about the clients. Inadequate interpretation of test results may lead to more questions than would no interpretation at all.

When they take personality tests, clients provide a great deal of information about themselves. They confront many issues that they may not have previously considered. All clients should receive an interpretation of their results in language that they can understand unless, for some compelling reason (e.g., they are tested in a personnel screening program whose size and test security requirements make individual interpretations utterly impractical), they agree in advance to forgo an interpretation of their results. In clinical contexts, interpretation of test results, when done correctly, may provide a useful therapeutic framework. In other words, the discussion of test indicators offers a basis for validating working hypotheses about the patient and leads to additional insights about the client's current functioning.

The use of a reputable test scoring service provides some assurance that the answer sheet will be processed correctly. Too often, the scoring of such instruments is left to inadequately trained assistants whose work is only cursorily reviewed. However, giving the client a copy of the report or profile designed for professional use is not recommended.

The test practice factors and elements do not directly address the issue of fees. However, charging for an interprofessional referral communication is likely to be viewed as double billing and unethical.

1. Comprehensive Assessment
7. Interpretive Feedback
3. Psychometric Knowledge
2. Proper Test Use

83. Being concerned with the individual differences of test takers, rather than presenting test scores directly from descriptions in the manual or computer printout.
78. Referring to a test as a basis for an interpretation only when the test has been properly administered and scored and the interpretation is well validated.
23. Skill in taking a good history to integrate with test results.
22. Knowledge of the need for multiple sources of convergent data.
71. Willingness to give interpretation and guidance to test takers in counseling situations.
53. Understanding the meaning of test scores in the pattern of evaluation.
15. Restricting test administration to qualified personnel.
12. Keeping scoring keys and test materials secure.
17. Knowledge of the test and its limitations.

63 What's a Percentile Rank?

SETTING AND APPLICATIONS

Education

INCIDENT

A high school student was sent by her parents to a private career counseling firm for assistance in choosing a college and in helping her plan her coursework. In accordance with the standard procedures of that firm, she completed an aptitude test and an interest inventory. The scoring procedure for the aptitude test generated a computer printout of her scores on the various subtests, expressed as percentile ranks. She was handed the results, but did not at the time receive any oral or written explanation of percentile ranks, nor interpretation of her particular scores. An appointment for test interpretation was to occur in 2 weeks.

Upon returning home, she looked over the printout and discovered that three of her scores on the aptitude test were in the 70th to 75th percentile range, the rest clustered between the 50th and 65th percentile. Because she was accustomed to interpreting test results according to the grading system used at her school, which was based on a numerical cut-off of 70% of items correct for passing, she interpreted her scores as "barely passing" or "failing" and became distressed. The next day, she went to her high school counselor because she was so despondent, whereupon she discovered that she had actually misconstrued the meaning of the scores.

FOCUS QUESTIONS

What procedures should be used to avoid misinterpretation of test scores?
What other information, in addition to the test scores, could be used to help the student with her educational planning?

In this case, the harmful consequences of improper test use did occur because the student became emotionally distressed by what she believed was the meaning of her test scores, which should have been released only in the context of a face-to-face meeting with a professional competent to interpret the tests used. The interpretation should have integrated the test results with other information such as school achievement and interests. The results of the test should have been released to the student only in the context of this interpretation. The harm done to this student could have been worse had she not sought and received appropriate information from her high school guidance counselor. The student or her parents might have made wrong decisions based on erroneous information.

Although percentile ranks are less difficult to interpret than many other types of normative scores, there is a danger that they will be misunderstood as indicating a pass/fail cut-off point. A percentile rank indicates the percentage of people taking the test who received a score less than or equal to the client's score. For example, a student who receives a percentile rank of 70 can conclude that about 70% of the students who took the test received a score equal to or lower than hers. Put another way, she would also know that only about 30% of the other students received a score that was higher than hers. A percentile rank of 70 does not mean that this student missed 30% of the items, nor does it signify a pass–fail cut-off point. Percentile rank in this context refers to the fact that the test taker is being compared with other test takers in a normative group; it does not refer in any way to the number of items on the test. It is also important when interpreting percentile ranks to make sure that the normative group on which they are based is an appropriate one with which to compare a particular student.

FACTORS INVOLVED

7. Interpretive Feedback
2. Proper Test Use
3. Psychometric Knowledge

ELEMENTS INVOLVED

46. Interpreting test results properly for the particular group tested, keeping in mind the characteristics of that group.
71. Willingness to give interpretation and guidance to test takers in counseling situations.
1. Accepting responsibility for competent use of the test.
2. Knowledge of professional ethics.
41. Understanding standard scores and percentile ranks.

64 CONDUCTING INDIVIDUAL ASSESSMENTS

SETTING AND APPLICATIONS

Employment

INCIDENT

A clinician in private practice was asked by corporation executives to examine their leading candidate for the position of regional sales manager. The candidate was performing well at the time in a middle-level management position for the company. The personnel director indicated only that the new job was a demanding one and that it required a person with a strong ability to cope with stress. The clinician did not conduct or obtain an independent analysis of the position. Neither did he request additional information or details about the nature of the position that caused stress.

The clinician conducted a 1-hour interview and administered a self-report inventory and a projective test. Based on these data, the consultant advised that the candidate did not have the necessary stress tolerance and would not perform adequately in the regional sales manager position. Upon receiving the report, the company promoted another individual into the position.

The unsuccessful applicant later requested a copy of the report from the clinician. The clinician refused. He reasoned that the company was his client, not the candidate, and that the report was confidential.

FOCUS QUESTIONS

Should the candidate receive feedback?
Did the clinician submit to management pressure to provide answers without an adequate foundation?

When clinicians use tests in employment settings, they need to know about special considerations in personnel selection. If they do not have the necessary expertise, they bear a responsibility to involve a professional who does.

The main issue has to do with the selection process. In this case, the clinician had not done the preparation and verification necessary to justify the final decision. His knowledge of the position and its demands was minimal. Extensive information about the job should have been obtained before designing the selection procedure. Solid job analysis information provides a foundation for understanding the demands of a job and planning appropriate assessment strategies.

The instruments used should bear a clear relationship to success in the job. Test users sometimes select tests because they are familiar with them, not because the tests are appropriate in a particular setting. The use of job analysis results and valid selection instruments lays the foundation for fair employment practices that benefit both the employer and employees.

The clinician correctly understood the consulting role as implying a loyalty to the company that paid for the services rendered. Unfortunately, the consultant did not understand that there is an obligation to examinees as well. The consultant may not be legally obligated to provide feedback to the candidate. However, there is a strong ethical responsibility unless some unusually compelling reason exists (e.g., company security). In such cases, the examiner should explain these circumstances before testing. By offering feedback to the candidate the consultant may have shared information that would not only satisfy the candidate's natural curiosity but also help the candidate improve.

FACTORS INVOLVED

2. Proper Test Use
7. Interpretive Feedback
1. Comprehensive Assessment

ELEMENTS INVOLVED

1. Accepting responsibility for competent use of the test.
2. Knowledge of professional ethics.
30. Resisting political pressures to shorten the planning, diagnostic, and interpretive process unduly.
67. Selecting tests appropriate to both the purpose of measurement and to the test takers.
71. Willingness to give interpretation and guidance to test takers.

65 THE WELL-MEANING TRAINER

SETTING AND APPLICATIONS

Counseling/Training

INCIDENT

A well-known organizational development consultant was asked to conduct a series of training workshops in the research and development division of a large high-tech company. The goal of the vice president of the division, who had contracted with the consultant, was to improve communication within a number of cross-functional product development teams that had recently been formed. As part of her intervention, the consultant administered the Myers-Briggs Type Indicator (MBTI) for the purpose of having the team members understand the different but equally valuable perspectives that each brought to the product development task.

The consultant scored the MBTIs and then conducted a 2-hour introductory training session during which she explained the theory of psychological type and its application to teamwork. Over the next few weeks, she met with each team member for individual feedback sessions during which she explained each person's results in detail and discussed with him or her the accuracy of the results.

With this foundation, the consultant stated in the next group session that she would now like the team to look at the implications of individual differences for team communication. She handed out a simulated product development problem and then broke the group into teams based on the similarity of their results on the MBTI. After the teams had worked on that problem, she re-formed the teams so that they were composed of individuals with very different preferences (based on their MBTI scores) and had them work on a similar problem. After these two exercises, she brought the teams back together to discuss their experience. To illustrate the effect of individual differences on communication, she revealed a flip chart that listed the type of each team member by name and then discussed the effectiveness of each team in solving the problem.

After completing this portion of the workshop, the consultant asked for feedback from the participants about the exercises. All agreed that the contrast between the two groups had been very useful in helping them see the impact of individual differences on group communication and effectiveness.

FOCUS QUESTION

How can test results be used in a group or organizational setting without violating confidentiality or without participants feeling pressured to reveal their results?

Even though the training exercise was considered successful by the consultant, the participants, and the vice president, this case does represent an example of test misuse that may often occur in the context of organizational training. The test misuse occurred when the trainer revealed the results of the each individual's MBTI without explicitly receiving permission from the participants to do so. She thus violated their right to confidentiality.

Although in this instance no participant complained about having such information revealed, and all found the exercises useful, proper test use would have necessitated that she receive explicit permission first, preferably during the individual sessions.

A less ideal, but more practical alternative in situations in which individual feedback sessions are not possible would be to explain to the group that for the maximum learning to occur, it would be helpful for each individual to volunteer their results to the group. This request would usually be made after the initial group interpretation of the MBTI so that the participants' consent would be informed. As a practical matter, most individuals choose to reveal their MBTI results when the proper care is taken to explain the terms in a positive and nonstereotypical manner.

Even this alternative, however, could still present a problem if any individual felt pressure from the group or the consultant to reveal his or her results. Another option then would be to form teams by first identifying the "type" of the various teams and then to allow participants to join any group of their choosing during either exercise. Although this might dilute the impact of the learning if many people chose this option, it is sometimes necessary.

FACTOR
INVOLVED

2. Proper Test Use

ELEMENT
INVOLVED

2. Knowledge of professional ethics.

66 THE RIGHT TEST IN THE WRONG WAY

SETTING AND APPLICATIONS

Mental Health

INCIDENT

A psychologist working with a multidisciplinary team on a psychiatric ward was asked to provide a personality assessment on a recently admitted patient. The case was discussed in a team meeting. The psychologist then left a Minnesota Multiphasic Personality Inventory (MMPI) test booklet and an answer sheet so that the nursing staff could administer the test to the patient. The psychologist also left instructions indicating that the patient should read the instructions in the booklet, complete the test on his own, and then return the test materials to the nursing station. Upon receiving the completed answer sheet, the psychologist scored and interpreted the MMPI in "cookbook" fashion (i.e., using only the MMPI data), employing an authoritative text. He provided oral and written reports to the team. He then had a brief meeting with the patient to discuss the results. In neither case did he put the "cookbook" interpretation into context based on other information available about the patient. Several months later, after an unsuccessful treatment program and discharge, the patient demanded the records of his hospitalization. Those records included the written report of the MMPI evaluation. Members of the multidisciplinary team, including the psychologist, were subsequently sued. One specific allegation was that the psychologist's report of the MMPI evaluation was inaccurate and did not fairly describe the patient.

FOCUS QUESTIONS

How should the psychologist have administered the MMPI?
What other factors might have been included in the reports to the patient and to the team?
How should the interests of the patient have been considered and protected?

The psychiatric ward was busy and the psychologist felt pressured to complete personality assessments (and all his other duties) in a hurry. His background in personality assessment was slim, and, in an effort to cope with all the demands on his time, the psychologist had altered his assessment practices from those he learned while in training. However, he was confident of his competence and rarely sought the help of his colleagues.

The psychologist was evidently fooled by the apparent simplicity of the MMPI compared with the projective techniques he was trained to use. He apparently failed to read the portion of his MMPI text dealing with test administration. Had he done so, he would have known that, although it was the appropriate for him to ask a member of the nursing staff to administer the MMPI, it was incumbent on him to make sure the staff member (a) explained to the patient the importance of the test results in his treatment; (b) ascertained that the patient understood the instructions for completing the test; (c) assured the patient that the results of the examination would be discussed with him; and (d) proctored the test administration. Faulty execution of *any* of these four steps—not to mention all four—could have invalidated the MMPI results, misleading the treatment team, and thereby contributed to the patient's unsuccessful treatment.

It is conceivable that the patient completed the MMPI properly in spite of the inadequate test administration procedures. However, the psychologist's interpretation of the test was also inadequate. Evidently, he also failed to read that portion of his MMPI text that discussed the importance of moderator variables such as gender, age, education, socioeconomic status, and setting in MMPI interpretation. Again, failure to consider any one of these variables— not to mention all of them—could have invalidated the psychologist's MMPI interpretation and thereby contributed to the patient's unsuccessful treatment. Furthermore, competent assessment requires the integration of the results of any test with extratest information about an individual's history and present status.

FACTORS INVOLVED

1. Comprehensive Assessment
7. Interpretive Feedback
2. Proper Test Use

ELEMENTS INVOLVED

78. Referring to a test as a basis for an interpretation only when the test has been properly administered and scored and the interpretation is well validated.
60. Establishing rapport with examinees to obtain accurate scores.
22. Knowledge of the need for multiple sources of convergent data.
72. Ability to give interpretation and guidance to test takers in counseling situations.
16. Using settings for testing that allow for optimum performance by the test takers.
3. Maintaining proper actions regardless of management pressures.
30. Resisting political pressures to shorten the planning, diagnostic, and interpretive process unduly.

67 Computer Feedback in Career Counseling

Setting and Applications

Counseling/Training

Incident

The vice president for personnel of a large manufacturer of personal computers was interested in implementing a comprehensive career development program for all employees. The VP wanted to include as part of this program the opportunity for employees to take assessment instruments, specifically, the Strong Interest Inventory (Strong) and the Myers-Briggs Type Indicator (MBTI).

The VP also wanted to take advantage of the high level of technology available at the company: Almost all of the employees had one of the company's computers on his or her desk. These desktop computers were all connected via a network that included electronic mail (E-mail) capability. E-mail allows any user to communicate in writing to any other user by typing the letter into the computer and then sending it to a particular person's electronic mailbox. The receiver can then read and respond whenever he or she checks for messages. All communication on the system is confidential: All electronic mailboxes are private and protected by secret passwords.

The publisher of the two assessment instruments was contacted to help set up the program. The plan was as follows: Software to administer the Strong and the MBTI on-line would be loaded onto a central computer in the career development office. All employees would be informed of the program and any employee who wanted to take either instrument would make the request on the computer, which would explain the purpose of the instruments and administer the items. When the individual had completed either or both instruments, the test would be scored by the computer and the results sent to the individual's private electronic mailbox, with a copy to a certified counselor in the career development office who was qualified to interpret either instrument. The results were in the form of computer-generated narratives that were written so as to be understood by nonprofessionals. Included with the results returned to the employee would be an offer to ask the counselor, via an E-mail message, any questions about the meaning of any of the results, or to call and make an appointment for a face-to-face feedback session with the counselor.

Focus Questions

Is this a professionally accepted practice?
Is a face-to-face interpretive session required?
If so, exactly what constitutes "face-to-face" communication?
What constitutes a professional consultation?
Do the potential benefits of career counseling via E-mail outweigh the potential harm?
What other information other than test scores might be useful in helping individuals with career concerns?

When this system was proposed, the counselor from the computer firm and a psychologist from the publisher met to discuss the issue of providing test results and interpretation via computer. Certain advantages to providing results in this way were identified. First, confidentiality was protected. In fact, with this system, client confidentiality was even greater than in a typical scenario in which the client makes an appointment and walks into the company counseling center. Second, there was no need to wait for an appointment, which, given the load in the counseling center, could take months to set up. Also, follow-up questions could be asked as they occurred to the client, at any time, simply by typing them into the computer and sending them to the counselor. The counselor could then take a few minutes, or as long as necessary, to answer the question, at any time that she chose. Third, if the counselor observed an unusual profile or was asked a question that she thought suggested a face-to-face interview, she could invite the individual to make an appointment. Fourth, the client receiving results via computer suffered no disadvantage regarding the printed results, as he or she would receive exactly the same interpretive material as would be provided to a client in an interview. Fifth, research on assessing lifestyle (see Allen & Skinner, 1987, pp. 111) has indicated that individuals are more likely to respond honestly to questions asked on the computer versus questions in person by an interviewer. Sixth, numerous research studies have demonstrated that clients enjoy taking tests on the computer, a finding likely to be particularly applicable to employees of this company, who were known for their commitment to the company's product. Seventh, use of this system could expose far more employees to the ideas of career development than would be possible if each were to have a personal interview with the counselor.

The following disadvantages were also noted. First, and most important, was the question about how comprehensive the interpretation could be if it were confined to test results only. Many personal and situational factors (e.g., hobbies, past experience, life roles, developmental level, and reasons for wanting to take a test) that otherwise could and should be integrated into an interpretation might not come to light with such a procedure. Second, there was a question as to whether or not interaction with the computer alone would be sufficient to help teach the client how to solve career-related problems. The goal of professional career counseling is not to provide information but to teach a process that the client can continue to use with future career questions. Third, the counselor would be unable to observe the client's nonverbal behavior, which sometimes suggests a difficulty in understanding parts of the interpretation, a negative emotional response to the information, or confusion. In a face-to-face interview, a counselor can note these behaviors and probe for more information, which can then be integrated into the feedback session. Fourth, any potentially contradictory information contained in the computer reports might not be addressed and resolved if the client did not ask about it specifically. A related question was, Would clients be less likely to request clarification via computer than in a face-to-face session with a counselor? Fifth, no prescreening was planned to determine whether the MBTI or the Strong—or any test—was appropriate, given the individual and his or her particular concerns. Sixth, because the administration of the instruments was conducted via the computer without the intervention of a trained administrator, what would happen if the client did not follow the directions?

FACTORS
INVOLVED

1. Comprehensive Assessment
7. Interpretive Feedback
2. Proper Test Use

ELEMENTS
INVOLVED

22. Knowledge of the need for multiple sources of convergent data.
23. Skill in taking a good history to integrate with test results.
60. Establishing rapport with examinees to obtain accurate scores.
77. Following up to get the facts from a client's background to integrate with test scores, as part of interpretation.
83. Being concerned with the individual differences of test takers, rather than presenting test scores directly from descriptions in the manual or computer printout.
73. Having enough sufficiently qualified staff to provide adequate counseling.
17. Knowledge of the test and its limitations.
61. Seeing that every examinee follows directions so that test scores are accurate.

Section 8

Administrative/Organizational Policy Issues

68 MISLEADING PUBLIC STATEMENTS

SETTING AND APPLICATIONS General

INCIDENT Promotional material for a commercially published test designed to assess honesty was misleading in that it suggested that it was the only test of its kind favorably reviewed in the *Mental Measurements Yearbook*. The promotional literature made no mention of the fact that subsequent editions of the *Yearbook* contain reviews of other commercially published psychological tests of honesty. In fact, at the time that the promotion took place, each edition of the *Yearbook* contained reviews only of those tests that had been introduced or revised since the previous edition, or of tests that had generated 20 or more references since the previous edition had been published. Thus, what the ad failed to mention by focusing on the most current version of the *Yearbook* was that reviews of other such instruments could exist in other editions of the *Yearbook*. In fact, in a later edition, other tests of honesty were reviewed, some favorably.

FOCUS QUESTIONS What procedures are needed by commercial test publishers to ensure that promotional activities are consonant with professional practice?

What steps can health care professionals who work for test publishers take to promote ethics in advertising?

Can you identify any other examples of advertising or promotion that might be misleading?

The person who developed the promotional materials failed to help the public make an informed judgment about the test materials by failing to disclose relevant facts. Laypersons are likely to believe what they read about tests; even trained professionals might be misled by such claims if they were not familiar with the publishing policies of particular sources of reviews.

One of the questions raised by this case is the role that psychologists and other testing professionals can and do play in the test publishing industry. Although very few test publishers have psychologists in the highest level positions, many publishers do have psychologists, psychometrists, or other measurement experts on staff. These individuals, however, often are assigned to product development, research, or editorial divisions within the company with consequently little or no authority to influence advertising or promotional activities. At the same time, they may be members of professional organizations with ethical codes that place their responsibility to their profession and the public higher than their responsibility to any particular organization. Such responsibility, without the accompanying authority, places these individuals in difficult situations within their own organization.

Ideally, test publishers should have formal mechanisms whereby consultation is sought from testing professionals about advertising and promotional material and policies.

Factors Involved
1. Comprehensive Assessment
2. Proper Test Use

Elements Involved
14. Evaluating tests and detecting misleading promotional material.
2. Knowledge of professional ethics.

69 ONE TEACHER'S RESPONSE TO THE "PERFECT" TESTING AND ACCOUNTABILITY SYSTEM

SETTING AND APPLICATIONS
Education

INCIDENT

A mid-sized city school district had for several years administered the same norm-referenced achievement battery in the fall in grades 2–9 to obtain information useful for instructional planning. A change in the school board membership together with increased national media attention about the poor showing of U.S. students in international comparative studies resulted in significant changes in the testing program as new procedures designed to raise achievement standards were implemented.

A second phase of norm-referenced achievement testing with a new test was added in the spring. As soon as the results were available, fall and spring percentile ranks (PR) were averaged for each student in each content area (e.g., reading, mathematics, and language). Local PR norms for both fall and spring were then computed separately for pupils, classrooms, and buildings; these norms were used without revision in subsequent years. Local norms for pupils were used to set a minimum standard for school grade promotion; local norms for classroom averages were used by administrators to judge the performance of teachers, including the awarding of bonuses; and local building norms were used to determine both the effectiveness of building principals and their salary bonuses.

The school board and central administration were pleased with their tight lock-step accountability and evaluation system. At the end of the third year, the superintendent proclaimed the success of the district's efforts by citing a decrease in the number of pupils retained and increases in the grade and building average scores on the achievement tests.

In a school that drew its students from both the inner city and the more affluent suburban areas, there was one "problem" class with a large number of inner-city minority children, all with limited reading and language skills. All attempts to teach this class had failed until a master teacher volunteered to take charge. Although he accomplished a great deal during his first year, he was unable to raise achievement test scores appreciably. During his second year, the class showed a dramatic gain over the preceding year, and the success of his teaching methods was widely advertised. During his third year, however, the teacher's real methods were exposed when a central office supervisor paid an unannounced visit and found him teaching actual test items from the forthcoming spring achievement test. Further investigation revealed that his students had copied answers and that these "crib sheets" were to be used during the test. The teacher was immediately fired, but he protested that he had acted in the best interests of his pupils, who were the victims of a grossly unfair testing and evaluation process, and that he had done no more than other teachers to "beat" such a reprehensible system.

Parents, teachers, and the general public all rushed to the teacher's defense. At the next school board meeting, he was portrayed as a hero by his supporters. In a newspaper editorial published after the meeting, he was described as a dedicated individual who had volunteered to help those less fortunate but who ended up being the victim of a misguided accountability and evaluation system. The negative publicity created by the case further depressed teacher morale throughout the district and created a huge public relations problem for the school board. Additional editorials and letters in the local newspapers attempted to define the cause of the teacher's difficulties and suggest remedies to the local school administrators.

FOCUS QUESTIONS

What erroneous assumptions did the school district administrative personnel make in establishing their assessment/accountability system?

What mistakes were made in the use of norm-referenced tests in this assessment/accountability system?

Were the teacher's actions justified? Why or why not?

What actions need to be taken to change and improve the system?

The school board and central administrative staff committed a number of egregious errors that culminated in this case, eroded teacher morale, and created an embarrassing public relations problem. Mistakes made by the school board members and administrative staff are outlined in this analysis.

This case illustrates the point that a single assessment strategy cannot meet all assessment and accountability needs. For example, public accountability measures will most likely be of little help in making placement/retention decisions. The district placed far too much reliance on norm-referenced achievement tests. Use of such measures as the sole criterion for pupil retention, teacher evaluation, and school effectiveness shows a complete lack of understanding of the nature and purpose of such tests. Although tests might be one source of information for student placement decisions, they should not be used to the exclusion of other information about performance on daily classwork, motivation, and a number of other factors that affect student performance and achievement. The use of tests in evaluating the effectiveness of teachers and principals and awarding them bonuses based on class or building test performance ignores a host of factors that influence pupil achievement. These factors include the attainment of goals not measured by multiple-choice achievement tests, the variability of achievement levels in a class or school, significant changes in students occurring during the course of the school year, and parental involvement and support of the school program, to name but a few. Test scores cannot account for the student, societal, and school characteristics that greatly influence learning outcomes, nor is there a way to determine the separate effect of each.

District personnel also committed a number of specific procedural errors in the use of the tests. Different achievement batteries should not have been used in the fall and spring. If the district was attempting to measure gains in student achievement during the school year, then alternate forms of the *same* test series should have been used to ensure continuity in the skills and content domains measured by the test; national norms comparisons cannot be made across different tests normed on different samples of students. Averaging the fall and spring percentile ranks resulted in meaningless information because percentile ranks should not be averaged. Moreover, such a practice masks any significant changes in fall-to-spring performance that should be of interest to educators.

The conditions surrounding the district's use of achievement tests were such that teachers and administrators were highly motivated to "teach to the tests." Although such unprofessional conduct can never be condoned, the school board and central administrative staff created a situation that was conducive to such a practice, especially in view of the strong and widespread condemnation of the system as unfair. This perception of unfairness can cause even highly professional teachers to take such action. When test results are used in isolation to make high-stakes decisions, teachers are easily tempted to engage in various forms of instruction based on actual test items. The school district in this incident took no precautions to keep the test forms secure or to rotate test forms on a random basis. Lack of security precautions made teaching the test items easy. It seems quite likely that many teachers were using the tests improperly because the district's performance was creeping upward each year. Such positive changes in performance are often attributable to repeated use of the same tests and aging norms, not real growth in student achievement.

As a teacher of students with linguistic disabilities, the teacher mentioned was placed in an unusually difficult situation because his pupils were evaluated by the same process as students in regular classes. Such special classes should be exempt from tests that directly penalize students for not having fundamental skills such as adequate reading ability or language facility, which are needed on most group achievement tests. Although the teacher's conduct was unprofessional and cannot be excused, some blame for the incident in his class (and in others) must be shared by the school board and central administrative staff. Until a number of fundamental problem practices are corrected, it seems likely that such irregularities will continue.

The school district could have been saved from an embarrassing public relations problem had it clearly established the desired learning outcomes with teacher participation and publicized these before any sort of testing program was instituted. If these learning outcomes had then been used to develop an appropriate testing system—for example, one based on locally developed tests—the role of testing could have been presented in a more positive light, particularly if teacher evaluation were not dependent on the results of such tests.

1. Comprehensive Assessment
2. Proper Test Use
3. Psychometric Knowledge
4. Maintaining Integrity of Test Results

34. Considering whether the reason for giving a test locally meets the purpose for which the test was designed.
6. Refraining from coaching or training individuals or groups on test items, which results in misrepresentation of the person's abilities and competencies.
2. Knowledge of professional ethics.
3. Maintaining proper actions regardless of management pressures.
13. Refraining from modifying prescribed administration procedures to adapt to particular individuals.
11. Preventing individuals from reviewing actual tests prior to administration.
9. Resisting pressures to amass higher scores than justified to make the system "look good."
19. Basing promotion/retention decisions, grades, or class assignments on wider information than a test score.
39. Advising administrators about the limitations of norms, especially grade equivalents, for student populations differing markedly from the norm sample.
25. Understanding norms and their limitations.
41. Understanding standard scores and percentile ranks.
52. Understanding statistical data in the pattern of evaluation.

70 A CASE OF SPEEDY SELECTION

SETTING AND APPLICATIONS Employment

INCIDENT John Smith, human resources director for a growing West Coast manufacturing company, administered the California Psychological Inventory (CPI) to assess candidates for promotion to senior management positions within an organization. The CPI results, which Smith accepted uncritically, were the only information used in making the promotion decision. Smith was not familiar with research evidence suggesting that specific family or work stresses present at the time of testing affect test profiles. He administered no other inventories and considered no other appropriate evidence, such as performance ratings. Smith used the CPI alone because the company president wanted to announce the promotions immediately. Smith recommended that a job analysis of the organization's senior management positions be conducted before the CPI was used so that the scales of the inventory could be linked to job requirements. However, management rejected this recommendation because the linkage appeared obvious. Testing proceeded rapidly because of the tight time frame within which to announce the promotions.

FOCUS QUESTION How can human resource personnel educate management regarding proper use of tests in employment testing?

This case raises broad questions about the human resources director's competency to administer and interpret the CPI. In addition, this case highlights two specific issues relevant to test misuse.

First, on what basis should decisions be made about individuals? Although test scores may be valid for particular applications, they should never be the sole source of information, because they are never perfectly predictive of an individual's behavior. All test scores contain some error. In addition, they represent an individual's behavior (in the form of responses to the test items) at only one point in time. Finally, it would not be unusual to see scores on the same individual differ as a function of the testing context (e.g., if the results were being used for selection rather than to provide career guidance).

For these reasons, other information should be integrated into a larger composite portrait of an individual before making a decision. Such information could include scores on other tests, job-relevant experience, employment references, and interview data. The task in selection is to determine if the applicant has the knowledges, skills, abilities, and other characteristics to perform essential position tasks successfully. No one test score can provide all this information.

The second issue of specific test misuse relevant to this case is that the human resources director failed to resist management pressure and compromised the selection procedure. People who assume the responsibility for test use have obligations that extend beyond the short-term implications of the moment. They have a responsibility to the test taker, other members of their profession, and to the longer term interests of the organization they serve.

Hiring an unqualified individual carries additional risks for the examinee. If the individual is unqualified, he or she probably will experience unnecessary stress in the position and possibly a sense of failure that could affect his or her self-esteem.

FACTORS
INVOLVED

1. Comprehensive Assessment
2. Proper Test Use

ELEMENTS
INVOLVED

3. Maintaining proper actions regardless of management pressures.
22. Knowledge of the need for multiple sources of convergent data.
23. Skill in taking a good history to integrate with test results.
30. Resisting political pressures to shorten the planning, diagnostic, and interpretive process unduly.

71 SELECTING DOCTORAL STUDENTS AT BEST STATE UNIVERSITY

SETTING AND
APPLICATIONS

Education

INCIDENT

One department at Best State University (BSU) admits doctoral students by having a committee composed of faculty members screen all applicants. The criterion used to determine admission to the program is an undergraduate grade point average (GPA) of 3.3 out of a possible 4.0. Applicants are not told exactly how the GPA is used in the admissions process. In addition, all applicants are required to present scores on the Graduate Record Examination (GRE) "for research purposes," even though the results are neither considered in the admissions process nor used for research purposes. The GRE is required by the department only because it is required by several leading departments at competing institutions as well as in other departments at BSU.

The chair of the faculty admissions committee noted the following data contained in the applications of two recent candidates for admission: Candidate A, who had earned a GPA of 3.4, obtained scores of 230 and 270 on the Verbal and Quantitative portions, respectively, of the GRE, for a total score of 500. Candidate B, who had a GPA of 3.1, scored 570 and 580 on the Verbal and Quantitative portions, for a total score of 1150.

Candidate A had attended a small "open admissions" college with mediocre academic standards, while Candidate B had attended a leading university noted for faculty research and the rigor of its academic program. Candidate A was admitted because the GPA admissions requirement was met; Candidate B was denied admission due to failure to meet the GPA requirement. As stated above, the GRE results were not considered due to department policy. After entering the doctoral program, Candidate A had demonstrated very poor performance in first-year courses; in fact, the student had become very discouraged before the end of the year and did not complete the second semester. Because similar cases had occurred in the past, the admissions committee chair became concerned about the GPA as the sole requirement for admission and sought assistance from the head of the University Testing Service.

**FOCUS
QUESTIONS**

What errors did the BSU department make in its use of admissions criteria to select graduate students?

How should test results and the undergraduate scholastic record be used in selecting graduate students?

Besides test scores and undergraduate grades, what are other possible criteria that might be useful in predicting success in graduate study?

This department had committed several errors in the admissions selection process used to admit graduate students. The GRE should not have been required of students if results were not used in the admissions selection process; moreover, the department should have been open with students about how the admissions requirements were used in the selection process. To require the GRE only because other departments or institutions do so is poor practice.

Although the undergraduate GPA is likely to be helpful in selection, it should not be used as the sole criterion with the application of a rigid cut-off requirement. The GPA in those undergraduate courses most directly related to the intended graduate major would probably be more helpful if such information were available. The BSU admissions committee should certainly have considered the types of institutions where the grades of the two applicants were obtained. It is likely that differences in grading policies and types of students enrolled at the colleges attended by the applicants made comparing GPAs from the two institutions difficult if not impossible.

The GRE results, unlike the GPAs, can be compared directly for the two candidates and are intended to overcome some of the difficulties encountered in comparing GPAs from different colleges having different grading standards. If the BSU admissions committee had considered the GRE results of the applicants, this would have provided useful additional information in the decision-making process. In the future, the department might want to consider using the GRE (or other appropriate equivalent) in the admissions selection process along with other criteria. Under no circumstances should a rigid cut-off be required on the GRE to the exclusion of all other information about a candidate.

Multiple criteria should have been used to select students. Among these are undergraduate GPA, GRE or other appropriate test results, letters of recommendation, and faculty interviews, if possible. No single criterion should be used to the exclusion of all others. If feasible, local research studies could be conducted to determine the predictive value of such criteria singly and in combination with one another. In the case of the BSU department, the University Testing Service staff should have the training to help plan and execute such studies.

FACTORS INVOLVED

1. Comprehensive Assessment
3. Psychometric Knowledge
6. Appropriate Use of Norms

ELEMENTS INVOLVED

22. Knowledge of the need for multiple sources of convergent data.
52. Understanding statistical data in the pattern of evaluation.
27. Appreciating the implications of test validity.
53. Understanding the meaning of test scores in the pattern of evaluation.
36. Considering cut scores based on validity data as well as on profiles.

72 OLD NORMS IN EDUCATIONAL ACHIEVEMENT TESTING

SETTING AND APPLICATIONS

Education

INCIDENT

A school district selected its current achievement test series in 1980 by having a committee composed of teachers, administrators, and testing staff conduct a thorough review of the major published norm-referenced achievement batteries. The test series was selected because it provided the best match to the curriculum objectives of the school district, and its standardization and technical properties were outstanding. The school district had at the time accumulated 10 years of data on student achievement in the basic skill areas with the same test form and the same national and local norms. When the newly hired testing specialist reviewed the current testing program, she knew that several changes were needed. After a preliminary discussion with the superintendent, selected principals, and teachers, she realized that a proposal to replace the current achievement test series with the most recent edition would not be a popular course of action. The superintendent was satisfied with the current testing program because student performance had improved steadily over the previous 5 years, and the superintendent enjoyed his reputation as a successful, dynamic leader, whose curriculum reforms had improved student achievement. Principals also enjoyed basking in the success of their teachers and pupils and were reluctant to change tests. Despite the fact that test content no longer accurately matched curricular emphases, teachers were definitely opposed to the idea of changing tests, because they felt comfortable with the current test. In fact, many teachers had photocopies of the test in their desks, and these were used as a reference for developing lesson plans and worksheets. The new testing specialist realized that she faced a difficult task in convincing school personnel of the need for a replacement test.

FOCUS QUESTIONS

What changes does the new testing specialist need to make in the testing program? Why?
Why does a steady improvement in achievement test results for a school district not necessarily mean there has been a real gain in student achievement?
What is meant by "teaching to the test," and why is it *not* recommended?

The school district's testing program had long ceased to provide useful, accurate information about pupil achievement for several reasons.

The test series, despite its technical excellence, was more than 10 years old, which meant that the national norms provided were based on pupil performance in the late 1970s. Thus, the school district's pupils in 1990 were being compared with pupils tested in the late 1970s, and it seems safe to say that the norms no longer provided up-to-date, descriptive information about pupil achievement. Also, the test content no longer reflected current curricular emphases due to the age of the test. Although using norms from the late 1970s might provide an interesting baseline against which to study changes in achievement over time, inferences from the test data would be difficult for several reasons, including the following: (a) The tests were not kept secure, (b) the general level of pupil achievement had not remained constant since the late 1970s, and (c) local curricular emphases had changed.

A second problem relates to lack of test security. Teachers had made photocopies of the test and used these for teaching purposes. Not only is photocopying test items unethical, but it is also illegal because it violates copyright law provisions. The steady improvement in scores observed over the previous 5 years probably could not be attributed to real changes in achievement; it might simply mean that teachers were teaching the test items well. No meaningful conclusions could be drawn from test data gathered under such conditions. It is appropriate for teachers to teach the concepts and skills measured by an achievement test, but not to teach the actual items.

The new testing specialist faced a number of real challenges. In order to conduct an effective testing program, she would have to (a) replace the test series with a new edition or an entirely new test; (b) use alternate test forms on a random basis; (c) implement strict test security measures and "educate" teachers about the problems that result from teaching to the test and the illegality of making photocopies of tests; and (d) "educate" the super-intendent, administrative staff, and teachers about proper use of achievement tests and how to devise a testing program that would provide the type of information the district needed to determine its pupil achievement accurately and evaluate the effectiveness of its curriculum.

FACTORS INVOLVED

2. Proper Test Use
3. Psychometric Knowledge
4. Maintaining Integrity of Test Results

ELEMENTS INVOLVED

4. Not making photocopies of copyrighted materials.
6. Refraining from coaching or training individuals or groups on test items, which results in misrepresentation of the person's abilities and competencies.
8. Providing appropriate training and quality control over operations for all users of tests and test results.
9. Resisting pressures to amass higher scores than justified to make the system "look good."
11. Preventing individuals from reviewing actual tests prior to administration.
12. Keeping scoring keys and test materials secure.
25. Understanding norms and their limitations.
34. Considering whether the reason for giving a test locally meets the purpose for which the test was designed.

73 INAPPROPRIATE CALCULATIONS AFFECT INTERPRETATION

SETTING AND APPLICATIONS

Speech-Language-Hearing

INCIDENT

A public school speech-language pathologist was using the Porch Index of Communicative Ability in Children (PICAC) in an attempt to determine whether a third-grade boy was eligible for speech and language treatment in an elementary school setting. She had a large caseload and had been encouraged not to spend too much time in testing, so she decided to omit the seven graphic subtests of the PICAC battery, reducing it to 13 subtests. When the testing was completed, the clinician added up the 13 subtest scores and divided by 13 to get an Overall (OA) mean for the battery. She then converted this OA mean score to a percentile score, using an OA percentile table in the manual. She determined that the child scored at the 28th percentile, which placed him within normal limits. Therefore, he could not be considered to have a communication disorder or to be eligible for speech and language treatment.

FOCUS QUESTIONS

Can shortening the length of a test battery compromise the validity of its results even though multiple tests remain in the battery?

What are the potential dangers to basing a decision about the need for special services on a single test battery score?

This clinician violated several important psychometric principles. First, she succumbed to pressure from her superiors to shorten her testing time. Second, she lacked enough psychometric knowledge to realize that by deleting some of the battery subtests, she could no longer compute the Overall (OA) mean for a partially completed battery. Because she omitted the more difficult subtests, which if included would have lowered the OA mean, she ended up with a spuriously high battery percentile score. This score was subsequently used as the basis for considering the boy's communication performance to be within the range of normal, which may have inappropriately excluded him from treatment. This clinician was also unaware that shortening a test can reduce its reliability and increase the possibility of errors in interpretation. Third, the clinician attempted to make an important clinical placement decision on the basis of a single test rather than by using a comprehensive assessment containing multiple tests.

The potential harm of the test misuse in this case was to deprive a client of speech and language treatment because of the misinterpretation of the test results. In addition, the abbreviated test battery failed to obtain an adequate sample of the client's abilities and weaknesses and led to a misdiagnosis.

Errors of this type rarely result from intentional efforts to alter testing outcomes. This clinician seemed to lack adequate psychometric training to realize the statistical errors she was making and how they might affect the test interpretation. With more psychometric knowledge and experience, she might have taken the responsibility for using the test properly and for adhering to the procedures specified in the test manuals. Finally, more training would have made her aware that important clinical decisions should not be based solely on a test score but should take all relevant information into consideration.

FACTORS INVOLVED

1. Comprehensive Assessment
3. Psychometric Knowledge
4. Maintaining Integrity of Test Results

ELEMENTS INVOLVED

45. Choosing of tests sufficient to sample behaviors for a specific purpose.
30. Resisting political pressures to shorten the planning, diagnostic, and interpretive process unduly.
43. Understanding the relationship between validity and reliability.
47. Avoiding interpretation beyond the limits of the test.
52. Understanding statistical data in the pattern of evaluation.
19. Basing promotion/retention decisions, grades, or class assignments on wider information than a test score.

74 THE PRESTIGIOUS PRIVATE SCHOOL

SETTING AND APPLICATIONS

Education

INCIDENT

A well-known midwestern private secondary school publicized its college acceptance rates and the high performance of its juniors and seniors on the American College Testing (ACT) Assessment. Average scores together with score ranges were often the dominant theme in recruitment literature as well as in the school's alumni magazine and annual fund-raising material. Along with the ACT score information, there was usually a statement extolling the virtues of a diverse curriculum, superior teachers, and opportunities for individual attention, with a definite implication that its superior academic facilities resulted in high test scores. Such high scores on the ACT Assessment seemed even more remarkable in view of the fact that most students scored within the average range on a scholastic aptitude test required at the time of admission to the school.

During the sophomore year, all students took the P-ACT+, a preliminary version of the ACT Assessment. Counselors used the P-ACT+ results, in part, to schedule ACT Assessment test dates in the junior and senior years. Lower scoring students would be encouraged to take the ACT Assessment later in the school year so that their test results would be received too late to compile summary data for the recruitment, alumni, and fund-raising literature. As a general rule, students with P-ACT+ composite scores below the 50th percentile were steered to one of the later test dates, whereas students scoring above the 50th percentile were steered to an earlier ACT test date. The headmaster of the school supported the practice of the counselors because he gained considerable prestige from the superior showing of his students. Occasionally there were problems with lower scoring students needing earlier ACT test dates to meet early application deadlines; for the most part, however, the system worked well because the counselors had become adept at matching college admission application deadlines and P-ACT+ scores with ACT test dates. Sometimes mistakes would occur and a lower scoring student would submit an application too late due to a late ACT Assessment test date. Occasionally the counselors would "mysteriously" run out of ACT registration packets and some lower scoring P-ACT+ students would be forced to take the ACT Assessment at a later date.

FOCUS QUESTIONS

In what ways did the guidance counselors engage in unethical behavior with regard to the use of test results?
What harm could result from the counselors' actions?
What sort of profile of its students should such a school as this attempt to provide parents and the general public?

The guidance counselors and headmaster of this secondary school definitely engaged in unethical behavior in manipulating student test dates for the ACT Assessment in order to place the school in as favorable a light as possible in promotional literature highlighting the superior test performance of its students. The implied link between excellent facilities and high test scores was dishonest in view of the fact that a significant number of lower scoring students were not included in the score summary data.

The actions of the counselors also jeopardized some students' college applications when, by mistake, a student was steered to an ACT Assessment test date beyond a particular college application deadline. Such practices would eventually result in harm to students as well as foster the ill will of parents. The reputation of the school could be damaged severely if the counselors' actions were discovered and exposed to public scrutiny. In fact, the negative publicity generated by such unprofessional conduct could outweigh any real gains accruing from the positive publicity generated by high test scores.

School officials lacked a true understanding of the role of standardized tests such as the ACT Assessment in their school program. Test results certainly received too much emphasis in the promotional literature of the school. Other accomplishments of the student body should have been publicized in the literature prepared about the school. Prospective students and public supporters of the school should see a much broader profile of a student body than average test score performance data. The school counselors and headmaster apparently did not take into account such important determiners of college success as school grades and extracurricular accomplishments; they behaved as though test scores were the sole basis for admission, when such is rarely, if ever, the case.

FACTORS INVOLVED

1. Comprehensive Assessment
2. Proper Test Use
3. Psychometric Knowledge
4. Maintaining Integrity of Test Results

ELEMENTS INVOLVED

9. Resisting pressures to amass higher scores than justified to make the system "look good."
3. Maintaining proper actions regardless of management pressures.
2. Knowledge of professional ethics.
39. Advising administrators about the limitations of norms, especially grade equivalents, for student populations differing markedly from the norm sample.
18. Perceiving the score on a test as representing only one point in time, subject to change from experience.
44. Understanding standard errors of estimate and standard errors of measurement.
25. Understanding norms and their limitations.
8. Providing appropriate training and quality control over operations for all users of tests and test results.

$\square$ 75 SAYING TOO MUCH BASED ON TOO LITTLE

SETTING AND APPLICATIONS

Speech-Language-Hearing

INCIDENT

A 5-year, 8-month-old boy was referred for a speech and language evaluation by his preschool teacher because of her concerns about his language development. The school department had a limited time period following parental permission within which to complete testing. The speech-language pathologist administered the Peabody Picture Vocabulary Test–Revised (PPVT-R) and conducted an informal analysis of a sample of the child's spontaneous spoken language. The speech-language pathologist reported that the child demonstrated "no difficulty in listening, following directions, or retrieving specific words." However, she concluded that the child demonstrated significant difficulties in spoken language, based on her identification of six grammatical errors in the child's 50-word spontaneous language sample.

FOCUS QUESTIONS

What could have been done differently to avoid the testing problem seen in this case? What educational training might the speech-language pathologist use to convince the administration that shortening evaluation procedures does not save time in the long run?

ANALYSIS   Time pressures for completing testing or insufficient understanding of the purposes and limitations of the testing administered led this speech-language pathologist to compromise on the completion of a complete assessment of the child's language performance. Because the PPVT-R was the only measure of understanding language that the clinician administered, because she did not report other observations of the child's ability to understand, and because she did not observe the child in the classroom or relate the teacher's specific concerns, her report of the child's comprehension extended beyond the data presented. Judgment of an expressive language difficulty was based on information too limited in scope to warrant such a conclusion.

FACTOR INVOLVED   1. Comprehensive Assessment

ELEMENTS INVOLVED   22. Knowledge of the need for multiple sources of convergent data.
30. Resisting political pressures to shorten the planning, diagnostic, and interpretive process unduly.
47. Avoiding interpretation beyond the limits of the test.
82. Presenting or reporting "clinical" observations made during testing only if the test user supports the observations by adequate background and knowledge.

76 "MANAGED" REPORTING OF STANDARDIZED ACHIEVEMENT TEST RESULTS

SETTING AND APPLICATIONS　Education

INCIDENT　School superintendents and principals are under increasing pressure to document the improvement of their students in basic academic areas, such as reading, mathematics, and written expression. Periodic administration of norm-referenced achievement tests has commonly been the means for determining changes in skill levels for grade or age groups. The reporting of test results by grade and school as well as for the district as a whole focuses public attention on the meaning of the test results; moreover, changes in student performance on the tests are certain to be linked to educational programs and curricular emphases that are the responsibility of school administrators, especially the superintendent.

There have been some instances, particularly in large urban school districts, in which administrators have been charged with reporting test results selectively to the public for the alleged purpose of reflecting favorably on themselves and their leadership. Certain students with low achievement (e.g., chapter 1,[1] learning disabled, and other special education students) have, according to critics, been deliberately removed from the statistical analyses of test data in order to present student achievement in the best possible light. There are two fundamental ethical questions that each school district must decide: When is it appropriate to remove students from group analyses? and How should the adjusted student achievement data be reported to the public?

FOCUS QUESTIONS　When is it appropriate to exclude certain students from the group achievement testing program? Who should be excused or eliminated? When should the elimination occur—prior to testing, or after the tests are administered?

How should group summary data be reported when certain students have been eliminated?

---

[1]Chapter 1 is a provision of the 1965 National Elementary and Secondary Education Act that provides funds for local education authorities to establish programs and services for educationally disadvantaged students.

Principals and superintendents who manipulate the reporting of test data in order to make themselves look good must be held accountable for their actions despite heavy pressure to "produce" educational results. Decisions about which students to exclude from group analyses need careful thought and consideration before such action is taken. If any students are to be excluded from reporting, prior approval by the board of education seems the surest way for the superintendent to avoid some of the criticism; however, there is no guarantee that board approval will eliminate criticism once the results come under public scrutiny. As a general rule, it would seem appropriate to aggregate and report test results for those students who share a common learning experience (e.g., pupils who are in the same classroom, the same special class, or the same special program). It does seem consistent with sound test interpretation to report results separately for regular classes, special classes, or special programs where the tests were given. If test results must be aggregated to obtain a single result for an entire grade by district or building, users should follow the same inclusion–exclusion rules the publisher followed in norming the test. Such practice ensures comparability between local results and national norms.

All school district personnel share a responsibility for maintaining the integrity of school testing programs, whether it concerns the procedures for reporting test results to the public, maintaining test security, avoiding the teaching of specific test items, or other actions that vitiate the results of the testing program. School administrators should attempt to take into account other important determiners of pupil achievement such as home background, socioeconomic status, parent education, and family and neighborhood stability when they evaluate school and program effectiveness. Evaluations based solely on achievement test results should be avoided.

FACTORS INVOLVED

2. Proper Test Use
3. Psychometric Knowledge
4. Maintaining Integrity of Test Results

ELEMENTS INVOLVED

1. Accepting responsibility for competent use of the test.
9. Resisting pressures to amass higher scores than justified to make the system "look good."
3. Maintaining proper actions regardless of management pressures.
8. Providing appropriate training and quality control over operations for all users of tests and test results.
2. Knowledge of professional ethics.
25. Understanding norms and their limitations.
53. Understanding the meaning of test scores in the pattern of evaluation.
34. Considering whether the reason for giving a test locally meets the purpose for which the test was designed.

77 TESTING LIMITS

Employment

INCIDENT

The recently promoted chief executive officer (CEO) of a medium-sized service organization contacted two university professors at a nearby university and arranged a meeting to discuss their availability to consult on a human resource problem. The CEO framed the problem as the development of an assessment system that could select the "best" managers from among a pool of applicants and incumbents. The CEO defined *best* as the "most aggressive and competitive." As the meeting progressed, it became increasingly clear that the CEO was dissatisfied with certain incumbents.

Once the assessment system was designed, it was to be implemented by the CEO's staff. The potential consultants became concerned that this arrangement would not allow them to monitor system performance adequately. In addition, they felt that the real intent was to use the selection procedures as an excuse to fire incumbents. For these reasons, the two professors declined further involvement in the project.

FOCUS QUESTIONS

What kinds of techniques might the consultants have used to promote fair employment practices?

What steps might the consultants have taken to ensure that they could monitor the system on an ongoing basis?

Consultants who provide advice have an obligation to assure that those who will be affected by their work are treated fairly. By resigning from the project, the professors ensured that they would not be a party to a misuse of their work. However, they did not fully resolve the problem.

The consultants might have considered working with the CEO to develop procedures that would serve as alternatives to dismissal. Such procedures might include additional training, or transfer to other positions. The consultants also could have assisted management in identifying desired future directions for the organization and in minimizing the negative consequences associated with change.

The consultants could appropriately have worked with the company to develop a selection program as long as there was no intent to use the results inappropriately. The development of valid selection or placement procedures based on a careful needs analysis would have represented a positive contribution to the organization. The CEO's desire to have "aggressive and competitive" managers would have been worth exploring further and might have resulted in a more careful understanding of the company's needs. In short, the consultants could have attempted more aggressively to convince the CEO to proceed properly. If they failed, they would still be obligated to withdraw from the job.

FACTORS INVOLVED

2. Proper Test Use
1. Comprehensive Assessment

ELEMENTS INVOLVED

30. Resisting political pressures to shorten the planning, diagnostic, and interpretive process unduly.
26. Appreciating the limitations of content coverage.

78 THE SCHOLASTIC ASSESSMENT TESTS ARE NOT SUFFICIENT

SETTING AND APPLICATIONS

Education

INCIDENT

A small community college suddenly found itself under intense pressure from local politicians and the State Education Authority to raise admission standards. The college had always used high school grades, letters of recommendation, and a personal interview to select students for admission. Some students went on to 4-year colleges after completing the 2-year program, but many went to work in the community after graduation. A large number of students did not complete the 2-year program, and this caused the State Education Authority to become concerned.

After a lengthy meeting of the faculty and trustees, the community college decided to change its admissions policy radically. High school grades, letters of recommendation, and a personal interview were all discontinued in favor of the Scholastic Assessment Tests, formerly the Scholastic Aptitude Test (SAT). The new policy was viewed as a way to achieve an objective standard of high quality for admission. The community college officials also thought that the SAT would be helpful in their communication with the community because the single entrance requirement would be easier to explain.

After announcing the change in admissions policy, college officials were surprised to receive complaints from high school seniors and their parents as well as from professional testing experts. The college administrators were puzzled by the controversy generated by their change and wondered what steps to take next.

FOCUS QUESTIONS

What should the community college administration have done to gain a clearer understanding of the drop-out problem?

Should the SAT have been used as the sole criterion for admission?

In keeping with the mission of a community college, what kind of admissions screening procedures should be used?

Although everyone agreed that the community college had acted in good faith in an attempt to improve the quality of the students attending the school, the policy was flawed and the college was soon forced to change. The major problem with the new policy was the narrow scope of information it provided about prospective students. Adopting the SAT as the sole admissions requirement resulted in a loss of valuable information about admissions candidates from such sources as high school grades, letters of recommendation, and personal interviews. The SAT has demonstrated its validity for admissions selection, but high school grades have been found to be equally good, if not better, predictors of college success.

Before deciding to use the SAT as the sole basis for admission, the community college should have carefully defined its mission and specified the characteristics desired in its student body. Only then could meaningful and useful admissions criteria be determined. Use of the SAT as the sole criterion for admission is a misuse of the test. It is advisable to use multiple selection criteria, such as test scores, high school grades, letters of recommendation, and various biographical data. The community college should obtain this information from prospective students. A validity study should then be conducted to determine which of these are most useful in predicting success at the community college. Based on past results, it is likely that the best predictors would be a combination of SAT scores and high school grades. It is only by such careful research that meaningful admissions criteria consistent with the designated mission of the community college as approved by the State Education Authority could be developed.

FACTORS INVOLVED

1. Comprehensive Assessment
2. Proper Test Use

ELEMENTS INVOLVED

22. Knowledge of the need for multiple sources of convergent data.
3. Maintaining proper actions regardless of management pressures.
17. Knowledge of the test and its limitations.

APPENDIXES

APPENDIX A

Contributors of Incidents

For a variety of reasons, not all of the cases provided could be included in the final casebook. However, we are grateful to all contributors.

William H. Angoff
Phillip Ash
Nancy Baker
Judy Barnes
Philip B. Bowser
Martha K. Brennan
Lynda Ruth Campbell
W. Grant Dahlstrom
Judith Dawson
Pat Dexheimer
Sharla Douglas
Robert C. Droege
Erica Edelman
Francis J. Fishburne, Jr.
David Flaherty
Blake A. Frank
Michael Franzen

Dorothy Fruchter
Ronald Goldman
Kathy Y. Haaland
Gerald S. Hanna
E. Helmes
David J. Irvine
Randy W. Kamphaus
Alan S. Kaufman
John Knippa
Otto Kroeger
Barbara O. Lewis
Robert W. Lissitz
Jaime L. Loyola
David S. Martin
Rebecca McCauley
Pierre G. Meyer
Pat Miller

Robert B. Most
Monica Nahwegahbow
Mary Anne Nester
Maria Pennock-Román
Marjorie Ragosta
Roland T. Ramsay
Mark Rieke
Frederick A. Schrank
C. Paul Sparks
Dorothy Steffanic
Cathy Telzrow
Carol Bloomquist Traxler
Roberto Velasquez
McCay Vernon
Janet E. Wall
Donald Zytowski

APPENDIX B

Reviewers of Cases and the Casebook

Lewis Aiken*
Ralph A. Alexander
Anne Anastasi*
William H. Angoff
Richard D. Arvey
Michael D. Beck
Richard A. Berg
Michael Berk
Elizabeth B. Bizot
Ann E. Boehm
Brian Bolton
Gwyneth M. Boodoo*
Phillip B. Bowser
Barbara A. Brauer
Martha K. Brennan
Christine Browning
Kathryn Buckner
Lynda Ruth Campbell
Karen T. Carey
Raymond B. Cattell*
Jan Ciuccio
Lee J. Cronbach
Dorothea J. Crook*
Mark Daniel
Anthony J. Devito
John K. Ditiberio
Lloyd M. Dunn
Charles B. Eberly
Erica Edelman
Ruth B. Ekstrom
Patricia B. Elmore
Ellen Fagan
Michelle M. Ferketic
Joseph C. Finney
Francis J. Fishburne, Jr.
David Flannery
Michael Franzen
Joy A. Frechtling
Bruce Fretz
David A. Frisbie
Edith L. Garduk
Leo Goldman
Donald Ross Green
George A. Grisdale
Larney R. Gump
Terry B. Gutkin
James S. Gyurke
Kathy Y. Haaland
Edward H. Haertel

Jamie Haldeman
Ronald K. Hambleton
Gerald S. Hanna
Charles H. Hargis
Bert Hayslip, Jr.
Lawrence W. Hecht
James J. Hennesey
Matthew G. Hile
Sandra Hirsh
Richard W. Johnson
Joseph R. Kandor
Susan Karr
Gary G. Kay
Charlotte Kuh
Jean Kummerow
Paul LeMahieu
Joanne M. Lenke
Al Levin
Craig W. Linebaugh
Rodney L. Lowman
Erin H. Lujan
Frederick C. Markwardt
Raquel Martinez
Mark Maruish
Joseph D. Matarazzo
E. James Maxey
Rebecca McCauley
George McCloskey
Kevin S. McGrew
Douglas McRae
William A. Mehrens
Scott A. Meier
Stephen A. Morin
Robert B. Most
Kevin R. Murphy
Jane Myers
Mary Ann Nester
Charles L. Nicholson
Anthony J. Nitko
Diane Paul-Brown
Carolyn R. Payton
Barbara S. Plake*
Dale Prediger
Aurelio Prifitera
Janusz Przeorek
Naomi L. Quenk
Marjorie Ragosta
Richard R. Reilly
Susan Reilly

Daniel J. Reschly
Cecil R. Reynolds
Marvin Reznikoff
John A. Rheinhardt
Mark Rieke
Rodolfo Jose Rosado
James P. Sampson, Jr.
Jon Sandoval
Evonne Schaeffer
Leo M. Schell
Cynthia B. Schmeiser
Mary Kathleen Schratz
Wayne Secord
Douglas K. Smith
Joan L. Sonnenschein
Sara S. Sparrow
John T. Stewart
George Stricker
Irene Strum
Jeffrey L. Sugerman
James S. Terwilliger
Robert M. Thorndike
Murray Tondow
John Paul Tonetti
Carol Bloomquist Traxler
Georgiana Shick Tryon
Gloria Turner
Linda Tysl
Susana P. Urbina*
Mary Usher
C. David Vale
Roberto Velasquez
M. W. Wager
Janet E. Wall
Richard S. Wang
Genese Warr-Leeper
C. Edward Watkins
Lawrence G. Weiss
Carol Westby
Pat Nellor Wickwire
Jo Williams
Kathleen T. Williams
Paul Williams
Hilda Wing
Paula Woehlke
Peter Wolmut
Karen Zager
Irla Lee Zimmerman
Pat Zureich

*Reviewed only casebook format and structure.

APPENDIX C

Measurement Textbook Resources List

EDUCATIONAL AND PSYCHOLOGICAL MEASUREMENT TEXTBOOKS

Aiken, L. (1991). *Psychological testing and assessment* (7th ed.). Needham Heights, MA: Allyn & Bacon.

Anastasi, A. (1988). *Psychological testing* (6th ed.). New York: Macmillan.

Bauernfeind, R. H., Wickwire, P. N., & Reade, R. W. (1991). *Standardized tests: A practical handbook*. DeKalb, IL: D'Amore.

Bertrand, A., & Cebula, J. P. (1980). *Tests, measurements and evaluation: A developmental approach*. Reading, MA: Addison-Wesley.

Brown, F. M. (1981). *Measuring classroom achievement*. New York: Holt, Rinehart and Winston.

Carey, L. (1988). *Measuring and evaluating school learning*. Needham Heights, MA: Allyn & Bacon.

Cohen, R. J., Swerdlik, M. E., & Smith, D. J. (1992). *Psychological testing and assessment: An introduction to tests and measurement* (2nd ed.). Mountain View, CA: Mayfield.

Congelosi, J. S. (1982). *Measurement & evaluation: An inductive approach for teachers*. Dubuque, IA: William C. Brown.

Cronbach, L. J. (1990). *Essentials of psychological testing* (5th ed.). New York: Harper & Row.

Ebel, R. L., & Frisbie, D. A. (1986). *Essentials of educational measurement* (4th ed.). Englewood Cliffs, NJ: Prentice Hall.

Fleishman, E., & Riley, M. (1992). *Handbook of human abilities: Their definition, measurement, and job task requirements*. Palo Alto, CA: Consulting Psychologists Press.

Friedman, A. F., Webb, J. T., & Lewak, R. (1989). *Psychological assessment with the MMPI*. Hillsdale, NJ: Lawrence Erlbaum.

Graham, J. R., & Lilly, R. S. (1984). *Psychological testing*. Englewood Cliffs, NJ: Prentice Hall.

Gronlund, N. E., & Linn, R. L. (1990). *Measurement and evaluation in teaching* (6th ed.). New York: Macmillan.

Guion, R. M. (1965). *Personnel testing*. New York: McGraw-Hill.

Hanna, G. S. (1993). *Better teaching through better measurement*. Fort Worth, TX: Harcourt Brace Jovanovich.

Hopkins, K. D., Stanley, J. D., & Hopkins, B. R. (1990). *Educational and psychological measurement and evaluation* (7th ed.). Englewood Cliffs, NJ: Prentice Hall.

Kaplan, R. M., & Saccuzzo, D. P. (1982). *Psychological testing: Principles, applications, and issues*. Pacific Grove, CA: Brooks Cole.

Karmel, L. J. (1978). *Measurement and evaluation in the school*. New York: Macmillan.

Lewis, D. G. (1975). *Assessment in education*. New York: Halsted Press.

Lien, A. J., & Lien, H. S. (1980). *Measurement and evaluation of learning* (4th ed.). Dubuque, IA: William C. Brown.

Linn, R. L. (Ed.). (1988). *Educational measurement* (3rd ed.). Washington, DC: American Council on Education and National Council on Measurement in Education.

Lutterodt, S. A., & Grafinger, D. J. (1985). *Measurement and evaluation: Basic concepts*. Tulsa, OK: G. P. Publishing.

Mehrens, W. A., & Lehman, I. J. (1991). *Measurement and evaluation in education and psychology* (4th ed.). New York: Holt, Rinehart and Winston.

Murphy, K. R., & Davidshofer, C. O. (1991). *Psychological testing: Principles and applications* (2nd ed.). Englewood Cliffs, NJ: Prentice Hall.

Payne, D. A. (1992). *Measuring and evaluating educational outcomes*. New York: Merrill/Macmillan.

Sattler, J. M. (1988). *Assessment of children* (3rd ed.). San Diego: Jerome Sattler.

Sax, G. (1989). *Principles of educational and psychological measurement and evaluation* (3rd ed.). Belmont, CA: Wadsworth.

Siegel, M. (1987). *Psychological testing of children from early childhood through adolescence: A*

TUTWoG corresponded with the authors of the measurement textbooks listed herein to provide updates on the progress of the casebook and to solicit information needed to ensure that the casebook would be well articulated, with widely used measurement textbooks in psychology; education; special education; counseling and guidance; speech, language, and hearing; and marriage and family counseling.

psychodynamic approach. Madison, CT: International Universities Press.

Thorndike, R. M., Cunningham, G. K., Thorndike, R. L., & Hagen, E. P. (1991). *Measurement and evaluation in psychology and education* (5th ed.). New York: Macmillan.

Walsh, W. B. (1989). *Tests and measurements* (5th ed.). Englewood Cliffs, NJ: Prentice Hall.

Walsh, W. B., & Betz, N. E. (1990). *Tests and assessment* (2nd ed.). Englewood-Cliffs, NJ: Prentice Hall.

Wood, R. (1987). *Measurement and assessment in education and psychology.* Bristol, PA: Taylor & Francis.

COUNSELING AND GUIDANCE ASSESSMENT TEXTBOOKS

Hood, A. B., & Johnson, R. W. (1991). *Assessment in counseling: A guide to the use of psychological assessment procedures.* Alexandria, VA: American Association for Counseling and Development.

Seligman, L. (1993). *Assessment in developmental career counseling* (2nd ed.). Cranston, RI: Carroll Press.

Shertzer, B., & Linden, J. D. (1979). *Fundamentals of individual appraisal: Assessment techniques for counselors.* Boston: Houghton Mifflin.

Watkins, C. E., Jr., & Campbell, V. (Eds.). (1990). *Testing in counseling practice.* Hillsdale, NJ: Lawrence Erlbaum.

SPECIAL EDUCATION ASSESSMENT TEXTBOOKS

Bagnato, S. J., & Neisworth, J. T. (1991). *Assessment for early intervention: Best practices for professionals.* New York: Guilford.

Bagnato, S. J., Neisworth, J. T., & Munson, S. M. (1989). *Linking developmental assessment and early intervention: Curriculum-based prescriptions* (2nd ed.). Rockville, MD: Aspen.

Berdine, W. H., & Meyer, S. S. (1987). *Assessment in special education.* Glenview, IL: Scott Foresman.

Bolton, B. (Ed.). (1987). *Handbook of measurement and evaluation in rehabilitation.* Baltimore, MD: P. H. Brooks.

Bolton, B. (1988). *Special education and rehabilitation testing: Practical applications and test reviews.* Austin, TX: ProEd.

Hargis, C. H. (1987). *Curriculum-based assess-*

ment: A primer. Springfield, IL: Charles C. Thomas.

Karnes, F. A., & Collins, E. C. (1981). *Assessment in gifted education.* Springfield, IL: Charles C. Thomas.

Neisworth, J. T. (1982). *Assessment in special education.* Gaithersburg, MD: Aspen Publications.

Rotatori, A. F., & Fox, R. (1985). *Assessment for regular and special education teachers.* Austin, TX: ProEd.

Salvia, J., & Ysseldyke, J. (1991). *Assessment in special and remedial education* (5th ed.). Boston: Houghton Mifflin.

Slater, B. R., & Thomas, J. M. (1983). *Psychodiagnostic evaluation of children: A casebook approach.* New York: Teachers College Press.

Swallow, R. M. (Ed.). (1977). *Assessment for visually handicapped children and youth.* New York: American Foundation for the Blind.

Witt, J. C., Elliott, S. M., & Gresham, F. M. (1988). *Assessment of special children: Tests and the problem-solving process.* Glenview, IL: Scott, Foresman & Co.

Zigmond, N., Vallecorsa, A., & Silverman, R. (1983). *Assessment for instructional planning in special education.* Englewood Cliffs, NJ: Prentice Hall.

SPEECH, LANGUAGE, AND HEARING ASSESSMENT TEXTBOOKS

Calculator, S. N., & Bedrosian, J. L. (1988). *Communication assessment and intervention for adults with mental retardation.* Austin, TX: Pro-ED.

Creaghead, N. A., Newman, P. W., & Secord, W. A. (1989). *Assessment and remediation of articulatory and phonological disorders* (2nd ed.). New York: Macmillan.

Darley, F. L. (1964). *Diagnosis and appraisal of communication disorders.* Englewood Cliffs, NJ: Prentice Hall.

Darley, F. L. (Ed.). (1979). *Evaluation of appraisal techniques in speech and language pathology.* Reading, MA: Addison-Wesley.

Darley, F. L., & Spriestersbach, D. C. (1978). *Diagnostic methods in speech pathology* (2nd ed.). New York: Harper & Row.

Emerick, L. L., & Haynes, W. O. (1986). *Diagnosis and evaluation in speech pathology.* Englewood Cliffs, NJ: Prentice Hall.

King, R. R., & Berger, K. W. (1971). *Diagnostic assessment and counseling techniques for speech pathologists and audiologists.* Pittsburgh, PA: Stanwix House.

Lloyd, L. L. (Ed.). (1976). *Communication assessment and intervention strategies*. Baltimore, MD: University Park Press.

Meitus, I. J., & Weinberg, B. (Eds.). (1983). *Diagnosis in speech-language pathology*. Boston: Allyn & Brown.

Nation, J. E., & Aram, D. M. (1991). *Diagnosis of speech and language disorders* (2nd ed.). San Diego, CA: Singular.

Peterson, H. A., & Marquardt, T. P. (1981). *Appraisal and diagnosis of speech and language disorders*. Englewood Cliffs, NJ: Prentice Hall.

Shipley, K. G., & McAfee, J. G. (1992). *Assessment in speech-language pathology: A resource manual*. San Diego, CA: Singular Publishing Group.

Singh, S., & Lynch, J. (1978). *Diagnostic procedures in hearing, speech, and language*. Baltimore, MD: University Park Press.

MARRIAGE AND FAMILY COUNSELING ASSESSMENT TEXTBOOKS

Fredman, N., & Sherman, R. (1987). *Handbook of measurement for marriage and family therapy*. New York: Brunner/Mazel.

Grotevant, H., & Carlson, C. (1989). *Family assessment: A guide to methods and measures*. New York: Guilford.

Jacob, T., & Tennenbaum, D. (1988). *Family assessment: Rationale, methods, and future direction*. New York: Plenum.

APPENDIX D

Worksheet for Cross-Referencing Cases to Textbooks

Course _____ Instructor _____

Textbook _____ Publisher _____

Core Content Topic	Case Studies (by Number)	Textbook Chapter	Pages
Test Selection/Choice of Assessment Procedure	1, 4, 5, 11, 14, 17, 18, 19, 22, 27, 28, 29, 30, 31, 32, 33, 35, 36, 40, 44, 46, 49, 50, 51, 52, 53, 54, 55, 57, 59, 60, 68, 69, 70, 71, 72, 73, 75, 77, 78		
Test Administration/Scoring	1, 2, 4, 6, 9, 12, 13, 15, 17, 18, 19, 20, 21, 25, 26, 33, 34, 35, 36, 37, 38, 39, 40, 41, 42, 43, 44, 46, 49, 57, 60, 62, 66, 67, 72, 73, 74, 75, 76		
PSYCHOMETRICS			
Descriptive Statistics	14, 30, 69, 71, 73		
Types and Uses of Norms	4, 11, 14, 16, 24, 27, 29, 30, 34, 35, 36, 40, 44, 45, 46, 47, 52, 53, 57, 60, 61, 63, 69, 71, 72, 73, 74, 76		
Reliability	45, 47, 54, 73, 75		
Validity	2, 4, 11, 16, 21, 26, 27, 28, 29, 36, 38, 40, 41, 42, 43, 47, 49, 50, 55, 56, 57, 59, 60, 69, 71, 73, 75, 77, 78		
TYPES OF TESTS			
Educational Achievement	24, 28, 44, 45, 52, 54, 60, 69, 72, 76		
Employment	2, 6, 27, 33, 39, 42, 48, 55, 68, 77		
Group Scholastic Ability	43, 54, 56, 71, 74, 78		
Hearing	20, 38, 53, 60		
Individual Intelligence	5, 20, 35, 36, 46, 51, 53, 55, 58		
Interest	10, 50, 63, 67		
Multiple Abilities	34, 47, 50, 61, 63		
Neuropsychological	5, 16, 17, 18, 19, 31, 32, 40, 46, 58, 59		
Personality	1, 7, 11, 21, 22, 23, 48, 49, 57, 58, 62, 64, 65, 66, 67, 68, 70		
Projective	3, 5, 12, 13, 15, 64		
Readiness	30		
Speech/Language	14, 29, 30, 37, 53, 73, 75		

(continues on next page)

Core Content Topic	Case Studies (by Number)	Textbook Chapter	Pages
SPECIAL APPLICATIONS			
Testing Special Populations	28, 36, 76		
Gender	2, 47, 61		
Individuals with Disabilities	20, 25, 34, 36, 39, 40, 41, 42, 43, 53, 59, 60, 73, 75		
Minorities	2, 4, 14, 26, 30, 35, 56, 57, 69		
Reasonable Accommodations/ Modifications	20, 34, 39, 40, 41, 42, 43, 60		
Age Groups			
Preschool (0–5 years)	14, 29, 30, 53, 75		
School (6–18 years)	3, 4, 9, 12, 16, 20, 24, 25, 26, 35, 43, 44, 45, 47, 50, 51, 52, 53, 54, 56, 60, 61, 63, 69, 72, 73, 74, 76		
College (19–22 years)	1, 10, 15, 28, 49, 50, 74, 78		
Adult (23–64 years)	2, 5, 6, 7, 11, 17, 18, 21, 22, 23, 27, 28, 31, 32, 33, 34, 36, 39, 40, 41, 42, 48, 49, 55, 57, 58, 59, 62, 64, 65, 66, 67, 70, 71, 77		
Elderly (65+ years)	46		
Factors Influencing Test Results	4, 6, 9, 17, 20, 21, 25, 26, 33, 34, 35, 36, 37, 40, 41, 42, 43, 44, 46, 53, 54, 57, 58, 59, 60, 61, 62, 66, 69, 70, 71, 72, 73, 74, 75, 76, 78		
Test Translations	4, 35, 40, 57		
Legal/Ethical Considerations	1, 2, 3, 4, 5, 6, 7, 8, 9, 10, 12, 13, 15, 16, 18, 20, 23, 24, 26, 27, 39, 40, 41, 42, 43, 48, 49, 51, 53, 55, 56, 57, 62, 63, 64, 65, 66, 67, 68, 69, 72, 74, 76, 77		
Public Reporting of Test Results	14, 24, 27, 69, 74, 76		
MISCELLANEOUS TOPICS			
Use of Test Records	6, 30, 35, 44, 51		
Diagnostic Evaluation/ Interpretation	4, 5, 14, 18, 19, 29, 30, 31, 32, 35, 36, 37, 40, 45, 46, 48, 49, 50, 51, 53, 58, 59		
Planning Interventions	9, 14, 17, 18, 35, 45, 48, 60		
Psychological Screening	7, 11, 57		

THIS SHEET MAY BE PHOTOCOPIED AND DISTRIBUTED AS PART OF
THE COURSE SYLLABUS

APPENDIX E

The 86 Elements[1] of Competent Test Use

1. Accepting responsibility for competent use of the test.
2. Knowledge of professional ethics.
3. Maintaining proper actions regardless of management pressures.
4. Not making photocopies of copyrighted materials.
5. Knowledge of legal standards.
6. Refraining from coaching or training individuals or groups on test items, which results in misrepresentation of the person's abilities and competencies.
7. Refraining from helping a favored person get a good score.
8. Providing appropriate training and quality control over operations for all users of tests and test results (e.g., administrators, media personnel who disseminate test results, department heads, teachers, and social workers, as well as psychologists).
9. Resisting pressures to amass higher scores than justified to make the system "look good."
10. Being alert to test takers who show passive or aggressive nonparticipation.
11. Preventing individuals from reviewing actual tests prior to administration.
12. Keeping scoring keys and test materials secure.
13. Refraining from modifying prescribed administration procedures to adapt to particular individuals (e.g., reading test items to an individual, defining specific words in an item, or encouraging an individual to reconsider an answer).
14. Evaluating tests and detecting misleading promotional material.
15. Restricting test administration to qualified personnel.
16. Using settings for testing that allow for optimum performance by the test takers (e.g., adequate room).
17. Knowledge of the test and its limitations.
18. Perceiving the score on a test as representing only one point in time, subject to change from experience.
19. Basing promotion/retention decisions, grades, or class assignments on wider information than a test score.
20. Considering errors of measurement of a test score.
21. Recognizing that reliability coefficients apply to given time and do not imply fixed performance levels of test takers.
22. Knowledge of the need for multiple sources of convergent data.
23. Skill in taking a good history to integrate with test results.
24. Recognizing that although test scores are observed, knowledges, skills, abilities, and personal characteristics may be observed in performance but are only inferred from test scores.
25. Understanding norms and their limitations.
26. Appreciating the limitations of content coverage.
27. Appreciating the implications of test validity.
28. Keeping up with the field and checking one's own interpretations with others.
29. Applying principles of test theory and principles of test interpretation.
30. Resisting political pressures to shorten the planning, diagnostic, and interpretive process unduly.
31. Matching a person to a job on the basis of aptitude validities for an occupation rather than on differences in a client's aptitude profile.
32. Considering the standard error of measurement.
33. Taking into account conditions that cast doubt on using reported validity for a local situation.
34. Considering whether the reason for giving a test locally meets the purpose for which the test was designed.
35. Recognizing, in a clinical setting, when a patient's state has been misdiagnosed or has changed, and selecting suitable norms.
36. Considering cut scores based on validity data as well as on profiles.
37. In a teaching situation, making clear to students research evidence for interpretations other than those suggested in the manual, as well as the limitations of each interpretation.

---

[1] In order to use simpler language, the term *elements* was used instead of the term *subelements* (Primoff, 1975). Minor editorial changes were made in the elements (see Eyde, Moreland, et al., 1988) in this list. Furthermore, these elements were slightly modified to better illustrate the cases.

38. Keeping a record of all test data for follow-up, establishing trends, and understanding how the test works in the local situation.

39. Advising administrators about the limitations of norms, especially grade equivalents, for student populations differing markedly from the norm sample (e.g., inflated city-wide grade equivalents due to a policy of no out-of-level testing, resulting in chance level–grade equivalent conversions that are actually above the functional grade level of many students tested; use of school means for school effectiveness comparisons without regard for differences in student population; and combining scores across achievement tests).

40. Refraining from making evaluations from inappropriate tests (e.g., clinical evaluations made from nonclinical tests).

41. Understanding standard scores and percentile ranks.

42. Understanding construct validity.

43. Understanding the relationship between validity and reliability.

44. Understanding standard errors of estimate and standard errors of measurement.

45. Choosing tests sufficient to sample behaviors for a specific purpose (e.g., neuropsychological testing).

46. Interpreting test results properly for the particular group tested, keeping in mind the characteristics of that group.

47. Avoiding interpretation beyond the limits of the test.

48. Refraining from using a research version of a test without norms for a non-English-speaking group to make placement decisions for such a group.

49. Making clear that absolute cut-off scores imposed for placement in special programs for the gifted are questionable because they ignore measurement error.

50. Interpreting differences among scores in terms of the standard error concept.

51. Using information in addition to published norms when interpreting norms (e.g., where grade equivalent scores tend to inflate levels of functioning).

52. Understanding statistical data in the pattern of evaluation.

53. Understanding the meaning of test scores in the pattern of evaluation.

54. Based on valid information, taking account of those elements in a test that discriminate against certain populations.

55. Avoiding errors in scoring and recording.

56. Using checks on scoring accuracy.

57. Checking frequently during scoring to catch error.

58. Following scoring instructions.

59. Not assuming that a norm for one job applies to a different job (and not assuming that norms for one group automatically apply to other groups).

60. Establishing rapport with examinees to obtain accurate scores.

61. Seeing that every examinee follows directions so that test scores are accurate.

62. Refraining from using home-made answer sheets that do not align properly with strip keys.

63. Following timing instructions accurately, especially for short speeded tests.

64. Refraining from equating sex/race samples by adjusting norms to fit subsample results.

65. Giving standard directions as prescribed.

66. Refraining from answering questions from test takers in greater detail than the test manual permits.

67. Selecting tests appropriate to both the purpose of measurement and to the test takers.

68. Selecting tests that are as free from discrimination as possible, considering the standardization sample and the test-taker population.

69. Detecting and rejecting unvalidated norms in an unauthorized computer scoring program for a standardized test that is marketed with novel, "home-grown" norms to avoid copyright liability.

70. Detecting and rejecting errors and overstatements in English narratives produced by computer software.

71. Willingness to give interpretation and guidance to test takers in counseling situations.

72. Ability to give interpretation and guidance to test takers in counseling situations.

73. Having enough sufficiently qualified staff to provide adequate counseling.

74. Willingness to coordinate group sessions in test interpretation.

75. Interpreting test scores to parents and teachers, rather than simply transmitting scores labeling the child without considering compensating strengths and actual school performance.

76. Placing only qualified descriptions and recommendations, not the actual test scores, in a school main office file.

77. Following up to get the facts from a client's background to integrate with test scores, as part of interpretation.

78. Referring to a test as a basis for an interpretation only when the test has been properly administered and scored and the interpretation is well validated.

79. Refraining from referring to the test as a basis for interpretation when the test is used by a good clinician beyond well-validated interpretation but is in a cycle of hypothesis formation and hypothesis

testing as a basis for a clinical interview and case study.

80. Using a test in a cycle of hypothesis formation and testing beyond well-validated interpretation.

81. Refraining from assuming that anyone capable of routine administration of a test is also capable of interpreting the results.

82. Presenting or reporting "clinical" observations made during testing only if the test user supports the observations by adequate background and knowledge.

83. Being concerned with the individual differences of test takers, rather than presenting test scores directly from descriptions in the manual or computer printout.

84. Integrating the computer printout with other results rather than presenting the printout as a report.

85. Refraining from labeling people with personally derogatory terms like "dishonest" on the basis of a test score that lacks perfect validity.

86. Refraining from reporting scores to administrators without adequate interpretation.

APPENDIX F

Overview of the Activities of the Test User
Training Work Group

The Test User Training Work Group (TUTWoG), a working group of the Joint Committee on Testing Practices, began its work in April 1989, when it established the following mission statement:

> TUTWoG is a work group of the Joint Committee on Testing Practices, a collaborative effort of test publishers and professional associations to advance, in the public interest, the quality of testing practices. The purpose of TUTWoG is to design, develop, and disseminate empirically developed training materials that will lead to improved test use by members of its sponsoring organizations.
>
> Training materials will be designed in accordance with professional codes and standards regarding test use and will build on the critical incident data base regarding test use developed by TUQWoG. These materials will be designed for test users involved in continuing professional education and graduate training programs.

Throughout the project, TUTWoG worked with sponsoring organizations and their relevant subgroups and involved a large number of textbook authors, test publishers, test users, and other members of the testing community. Symposia were held in conjunction with the annual conventions of the sponsoring organizations (American Speech-Language-Hearing Association [ASHA], 1989; American Association for Counseling and Development [AACD], 1990; American Psychological Association [APA], 1990, 1992; National Association of School Psychologists [NASP], 1993), and briefings of top officials were held (APA, 1989, 1990, 1991; AACD, 1992; NASP, 1992; Association for Assessment in Counseling, 1993). In addition, the test user project was featured at the 1989 Spring Conference on Test User Qualifications and Test Use Ethics by the Personnel Testing Council of Southern California, and a symposium was held at the 1991 National Council on Measurement in Education [NCME] Annual Meeting. Furthermore, a symposium was presented at the 1990 International Congress of Applied Psychology in Kyoto, Japan.

TUTWoG began its work by conducting a needs survey of 218 test publishers, textbook authors, and test users. The potential consumers evaluated the desirability of preparing a casebook, training modules, or workshops. More than one third of these experts replied and enthusiastically supported the development of a casebook on good and poor testing practices. Many respondents volunteered to aid in the development of the casebook in capacities such as serving as reviewers of cases.

A continuing dialogue with textbook authors—ultimately including the writers of 67 texts in tests and measurement and in specialty testing listed in appendix C—was established with the objective of producing a casebook that would likely be used by educators and trainers. As a result, TUTWoG concluded that the casebook should be used as a supplement to textbooks on testing.

The cases used in this book are based on incidents that actually occurred or were adapted from a variety of sources, including cases published by the APA and the Society for Industrial and Organizational Psychology. One case was loosely adapted from a U.S. newspaper article. Critical incidents were solicited from sponsoring professional associations (e.g., ASHA and NASP, as noted earlier) through periodicals.

A draft article requesting cases was sent to newsletter editors of the following APA divisions: Evaluation, Measurement, and Statistics (5); Clinical Psychology (12); Society for Industrial and Organizational Psychology (14); School Psychology (16); Counseling Psychology (17); Psychologists in Public Service (18); Adult Development and Aging (20); Community Psychology (27); Psychotherapy (29); Psychology of Women (35); Clinical Neuropsychology (40); Psychologists in Independent Practice (42); Society for Psychological Study of Lesbian and Gay Issues (44); and the Society for the Psychological Study of Ethnic Minority Issues (45). All state psychological association ethics committees also were sent requests for critical incidents. Furthermore, test publishers and test users were also contacted.

A meeting was held with experts in teaching and leaders in educational, speech-language-hearing, counseling, and personnel testing, who were

---

See also material under Casebook Development and Comprehensive Case Coverage in chapter 1, page 4.

asked to comment on the content, format, and organization of the casebook. In particular, they were asked to respond to this question, How should the casebook materials be organized to promote learning or to facilitate teaching?

Several clinical and industrial–organizational cases were discussed at a colloquium held at the University of South Florida. Extensive comments on industrial–organizational cases were made by students at California State University at Long Beach.

Extensive discussions were held on the arrangement of the cases in the casebook. TUTWoG's initial inclination was to arrange the cases according to the setting/testing applications, such as an education or employment setting. This plan was rejected when we realized that this arrangement would not encourage persons to acquaint themselves with test misuse outside of their own specialty. Indeed, one of the major findings in the study in which we identified the factors and elements of test misuse (Eyde, Moreland, et al., 1988) was that similar types of test misuse occurred across settings. We also considered arranging the cases by test misuse factors, an idea that was rejected because of the large number of cases related to Factor 1 (Comprehensive Testing). Because the factors and elements in the cases are multidimensional, we chose to use extensive cross-referencing systems by setting, factor, and elements of test misuse and by textbook topics.

We finally chose to arrange the cases in the natural order in which testing occurs, because committee members with extensive teaching experience believed that this arrangement would facilitate use of the casebook in educational and training situations. We selected the location of each case in the testing process after a panel of independent raters sorted the cases into the categories and placed each case into the category most descriptive of its contents. The first category deals with general education and training needs, and the second category deals with cases related to training for professional responsibility. After these two training and education categories, cases are arranged according to the sequence generally followed in test use: test selection, test administration, test scoring and the mechanics of using norms, test interpretation, and reporting to clients.

The cases were arranged in the order presented in this book when the large-scale mailout to reviewers occurred. The reviewers were asked to rate the overall quality of the organization of the casebook and were requested to comment on any problems encountered with the organizational scheme of the casebook. The present organization received high ratings from the reviewers and few negative comments; thus the order of the cases by the testing process was retained.

Over 140 draft casebooks were distributed to test publishers, test authors, textbook authors, relevant committees (e.g., those dealing with disabilities), and other testing experts. The cases have been revised on the basis of comments received from more than 145 reviewers who completed more than 890 reviews of individual cases.

Cases were selected if they:

1. Described real-life, significant testing practices that could be encountered by test users.

2. Were relevant and of interest to most graduate students, instructors, and practitioners in most disciplines that use tests.

3. Were reported in an objective manner.

4. Were reported in a manner that reflected respect for all individuals and groups, regardless of physical, mental, emotional, political, economic, social, cultural, ethnic, racial, gender, sexual orientation, or religious characteristics. Furthermore, cases selected were reported by the submitter in a manner that reflected respect for all professions.

5. Were of an appropriate length and written in an appropriate style and format.

6. Were accurate and at an appropriate level of comprehensiveness and complexity.

7. Did not duplicate or have substantial overlap with other selected cases.

Reviewers were asked to evaluate the cases according to their comprehensiveness, accuracy, relevance, importance, and other characteristics. Cases were selected if they received high ratings by reviewers or they were revised until relatively high ratings were attained.

Nine cases that were submitted were not used. These cases failed to meet criteria 1, 2, 3, 5, 6, & 7. Also, cases that appeared to be libelous were excluded from the casebook.

APPENDIX G

Sample of Critical Incident Form Used in Test User
Training Work Group Research for *Responsible Test
Use: Case Studies for Assessing Human Behavior*

Test User Training Work Group
(TUTWoG)

Critical Incident Report

TITLE:

TEST:

INCIDENT:

FOCUS QUESTIONS:

ANALYSIS AND DISCUSSION:

MAJOR FACTOR AND SUBELEMENTS RANKED BY IMPORTANCE

TOPIC KEY TO TEXTBOOKS:
(to be completed later)

SUBMITTED BY: _____

ADDRESS: _____

_____

_____

(If you need more space, please attach sheets as needed)

Return by: _____   **to:**
Lorraine D. Eyde, PhD
℅ Science Directorate
American Psychological Association
750 First Street, NE
Washington, DC 20002-4242

INSTRUCTIONS FOR COMPLETING CRITICAL INCIDENT REPORT

Please follow these directions to complete the Critical Incident Report Sheet:

1. TITLE: Suggest a brief title that you feel describes the critical incident well.

2. TEST: List the test(s) involved in the critical incident.

3. CRITICAL INCIDENT: Give the basic details of the incident of test misuse. Describe briefly the setting in which the incident occurred, relevant background information concerning factors that led to the test misuse, the exact nature of the misuse, the individuals involved, and the consequences of the misuse. Be as brief as possible; if more space is required, attach an additional sheet of paper.

4. FOCUS QUESTIONS: List a few (two or three) major questions that will serve to highlight the type of misuse that occurred. These should focus the reader's attention on the main points to be made in discussing the case.

5. ANALYSIS AND DISCUSSION: Provide brief answers to the following three questions. These answers should also cover the major points to be made in answering the FOCUS QUESTIONS (#4 above):

   A. What led to the test misuse?
   B. What potential harm could result from this test misuse?
   C. What are possible solutions to the problem posed by this test misuse?

6. MAJOR FACTORS AND SUBELEMENTS RANKED BY IMPORTANCE: First, choose one or more factors of test misuse from the attached list. Next, choose the relevant subelements for the factor selected and list these in order of their judged importance.

7. Please give your name, address, and telephone number.

THANK YOU FOR YOUR ASSISTANCE

APPENDIX H

Casebook User Comment Form

The authors and publisher of *Responsible Test Use: Case Studies for Assessing Human Behavior* are interested in receiving your comments in order to improve the casebook for future users. **Users may wish to photocopy this form**, then complete and mail it to Lorraine D. Eyde, PhD, % Science Directorate, American Psychological Association, 750 First Street, NE, Washington, DC 20002-4242.

Please answer each question below:

1. Describe how the casebook was used and the course where used, if applicable:

2. How many case studies were used or assigned?

   How were these case studies selected?

3. The case studies are grouped in the casebook according to the testing process (e.g., training; administration and scoring). Was this organization useful?

   Yes _____ No _____

   If "No," what organization scheme would have been more useful for your purposes?

4. Did you use any of the alternate organization schemes?
   (Check the appropriate response.)

   Cases classified by setting/application? Yes _____ No _____

   Cases classified by factors of test misuse? Yes _____ No _____

   Cases classified by elements of competent test use? Yes _____ No _____

   Cases classified by general types of tests? Yes _____ No _____

   If another classification scheme is not currently offered but should be added, please describe it.

5. Did you use the system for cross-referencing cases to textbooks? Yes _____ No _____

    If "Yes," describe any benefits or problems.

    If "No," describe the system you did use to cross-reference case studies to textbooks.

    How can the cross-referencing scheme be improved?

6. List by number any case studies that you found especially useful.

7. List by number any case studies that presented problems of any sort and describe the problem.

8. Other comments:

NOTE: If you can share your textbook cross-referencing scheme with other casebook users, send a copy of the completed textbook cross-referencing worksheet (appendix D) with this questionnaire to Lorraine D. Eyde, PhD, % Science Directorate, American Psychological Association, 750 First Street NE, Washington DC 20002-4242; or, if you used a different cross-referencing system, please submit a description of your system.

APPENDIX I

Critical Incident Submission Form

We encourage you to submit incidents of good or poor test use for possible inclusion in future editions or supplements to *Responsible Test Use: Case Studies for Assessing Human Behavior*. Follow the directions given below to complete this form. Use additional sheets of paper if necessary. You may photocopy this form as needed. Return the completed form to Lorraine D. Eyde, PhD, % Science Directorate, American Psychological Association, 750 First Street, NE, Washington, DC 20002-4242.

1. Critical incident. Describe in 500 words or less an incident in which a test was used improperly or properly. Summarize the basic details of the incident. Describe briefly the setting in which the incident occurred, relevant background information, and the exact nature of good or poor test use.

2. Describe the consequences of the good or poor test use mentioned in the critical incident.

3. List the test(s) used in the critical incident.

4. Factors of proper test use ranked by importance. Consider the factors of proper test use listed in the left-hand column of Exhibit 1 on page 9. Choose one or more of the factors that are pertinent to the type of good or poor test use exemplified by the critical incident. If more than one of the factors applies to the case, rank the factors in the order of their importance.

5. Elements of competent test use ranked by importance. Consider the elements of competent test use given in appendix E. Choose one or more of the elements that are pertinent to the type of good or poor test use exemplified by the critical incident. If more than one of the elements applies to the case, rank the factors in the order of their importance.

6. Submitted by: _____

Address: _____

_____

_____

Telephone: _____

Please return completed forms to:

Lorraine D. Eyde, PhD
℅ Science Directorate
American Psychological Association
750 First Street, NE
Washington, DC 20002-4242

THIS FORM MAY BE PHOTOCOPIED AS NEEDED

APPENDIX J

Index of Cases by Setting and Applications

APPENDIX K

Index of Cases by Element

34. Considering whether the reason for giving a test locally meets the purpose for which the test was designed. *3, 27, 28, 44, 52, 57, 69, 72, 76*

35. Recognizing, in a clinical setting, when a patient's state has been misdiagnosed or has changed, and selecting suitable norms. *46, 53, 57*

36. Considering cut scores based on validity data as well as on profiles. *71*

38. Keeping a record of all test data for follow-up, establishing trends, and understanding how the test works in the local situation. *48*

39. Advising administrators about the limitations of norms, especially grade equivalents, for student populations differing markedly from the norm sample. *24, 69, 74*

40. Refraining from making evaluations from inappropriate tests. *5, 14, 30, 31, 36, 50, 55, 56*

41. Understanding standard scores and percentile ranks. *29, 44, 45, 52, 63, 69*

43. Understanding the relationship between validity and reliability. *73*

44. Understanding standard errors of estimate and standard errors of measurement. *30, 60, 61, 74*

45. Choosing tests sufficient to sample behaviors for a specific purpose. *4, 5, 14, 30, 31, 32, 35, 36, 46, 49, 50, 59, 73*

46. Interpreting test results properly for the particular group tested, keeping in mind the characteristics of that group. *14, 18, 27, 60, 61, 63*

47. Avoiding interpretation beyond the limits of the test. *4, 16, 19, 30, 31, 36, 50, 56, 73, 75*

48. Refraining from using a research version of a test without norms for a non-English-speaking group to make placement decisions for such a group. *16, 35*

49. Making clear that absolute cut-off scores imposed for placement in special programs for the gifted are questionable because they ignore measurement error. *54*

50. Interpreting differences among scores in terms of the standard error concept. *24, 45, 47*

52. Understanding statistical data in the pattern of evaluation. *57, 69, 71, 73*

53. Understanding the meaning of test scores in the pattern of evaluation. *4, 18, 24, 62, 71, 76*

54. Based on valid information, taking account of those elements in a test that discriminate against certain populations. *4, 57*

55. Avoiding errors in scoring and recording. *19*

59. Not assuming that a norm for one job applies to a different job. *27*

60. Establishing rapport with examinees to obtain accurate scores. *25, 43, 49, 66, 67*

61. Seeing that every examinee follows directions so that test scores are accurate. *2, 33, 35, 49, 67*

62. Refraining from using home-made answer sheets that do not align properly with strip keys. *6*

63. Following timing instructions accurately, especially for short speeded tests. *2, 6, 33*

64. Refraining from equating sex/race samples by adjusting norms to fit subsample results. *2*

65. Giving standard directions as prescribed. *2, 33, 34, 36, 38, 40*

67. Selecting tests appropriate to both the purpose of measurement and to the test takers. *4, 14, 22, 27, 30, 40, 41, 53, 57, 60, 64*

68. Selecting tests that are as free from discrimination as possible, considering the standardization sample and the test-taker population. *4, 14, 26, 57*

69. Detecting and rejecting unvalidated norms in an unauthorized computer scoring program for a standardized test that is marketed with novel, "home-grown" norms to avoid copyright liability. *16*

70. Detecting and rejecting errors and overstatements in English narratives produced by computer software. *11*

71. Willingness to give interpretation and guidance to test takers in counseling situations. *26, 48, 62, 63, 64*

72. Ability to give interpretation and guidance to test takers in counseling situations. *49, 66*

73. Having enough sufficiently qualified staff to provide adequate counseling. *67*

75. Interpreting test scores to parents and teachers, rather than simply transmitting scores labeling the child without considering compensating strengths and actual school performance. *51*

77. Following up to get the facts from a client's background to integrate with test scores, as part of interpretation. *67*

78. Referring to a test as a basis for an interpretation

only when the test has been properly administered and scored and the interpretation is well validated. *4, 16, 19, 21, 34, 36, 39, 40, 49, 62, 66*

82. Presenting or reporting "clinical" observations made during testing only if the test user supports the observations by adequate background and knowledge. *20, 75*

83. Being concerned with the individual differences of test takers, rather than presenting test scores directly from descriptions in the manual or computer printout. *11, 53, 62, 67*

84. Integrating the computer printout with other results rather than presenting the printout as a report. *11*

86. Refraining from reporting scores to administrators without adequate interpretation. *1, 14, 29, 35*

APPENDIX L

Index of Cases by Factor

REFERENCES

Allen, B., & Skinner, H. A. (1987). Lifestyle assessment using microcomputers. In J. N. Butcher (Ed.), *Computerized psychological assessment* (pp. 108–123). New York: Basic Books.

American Association for Counseling and Development. (1988). *Ethical standards.* Washington, DC: Author.

American Association for Counseling and Development. (1989, May 11). The responsibilities of test users. *Guidepost,* pp. 12, 16, 18, 27.

American Association of State Psychology Boards. (1991, May). *AASPB Code of Conduct.* Montgomery, AL: Author.

American Federation of Teachers, National Council on Measurement in Education, & National Education Association. (1990). *Standards for teacher competence in educational assessment of students.* Washington, DC: Author.

American Psychological Association. (1981). *Report on the Conference on Testing, Assessment and Public Policy, August 25, 1981.* Washington, DC: Author.

American Psychological Association. (1987a). *Casebook on ethical principles of psychologists.* Washington, DC: Author.

American Psychological Association Board of Professional Affairs, Committee on Professional Standards. (1987b). General guidelines for providers of psychological services. *American Psychologist, 42*(7), 712–723.

American Psychological Association. (1992a). Ethical principles of psychologists and code of conduct. *American Psychologist, 47,* 1597–1611. Washington, DC: Author.

American Psychological Association, Committee on Children, Youth and Families, Committee on Psychological Tests and Assessment, and Committee on Ethnic Minority Affairs. (1992b). *Psychological testing of language minority and culturally different children.* Washington, DC: American Psychological Association.

American Psychological Association, Committee on Ethical Standards for Psychology. (1950). Ethical standards for the distribution of psychological tests and diagnostic aids: Code of standards for test distribution. *American Psychologist, 5,* 620–626.

American Psychological Association, Committee on Professional Standards. (1984). Casebook for providers of psychological services. *American Psychologist, 39,* 663–668.

American Speech-Language-Hearing Association. (1991). *Code of ethics of the American Speech-Language-Hearing Association.* Rockville, MD: Author.

Anastasi, A. (1988). *Psychological testing* (6th ed.). New York: Macmillan.

Anastasi, A. (1989a). What is test misuse? Perspectives of a measurement expert. In Educational Testing Service (ETS) (Ed.), *The uses of standardized tests in American education* (pp. 15–25). Princeton, NJ: Educational Testing Service.

Anastasi, A. (1989b). Ability testing in the 1980's and beyond: Some major trends. *Public Personnel Management, 18,* 471–484.

Anastasi, A. (1992a). Introductory remarks. In K. F. Geisinger, (Ed.), *Psychological testing of Hispanics* (pp. 1–7). Washington, DC: American Psychological Association.

Anastasi, A. (1992b). Tests and assessment. What counselors should know about the use and interpretation of psychological tests. *Journal of Counseling and Development, 70,* 610–615.

Anastasi, A. (1993). A century of psychological testing: Origins, problems, and progress. In T. K. Fagan & G. R. VandenBos (Eds.), *Exploring Applied Psychology: Origins and Critical Analyses* (pp. 11–36). Washington, DC: American Psychological Association.

Association for Psychological Type. (Undated a). *Ethical principles.* Kansas City, MO: Author.

Association for Psychological Type. (Undated b). *Special reminders and suggestions for using the MBTI.* Kansas City, MO: Author.

Bond, L., Camara, W., & VandenBos, G. R. (1989). Psychological test standards and clinical practice. *Hospital and Community Psychiatry, 40,* 687.

Carter, L. F. (1965). Psychological tests and public responsibility: Introduction. *American Psychologist, 20,* 123–124.

Cohen R. J., Swerdlik, M. E., & Smith, D. J. (1992). *Psychological testing: An introduction to tests and measurements.* Mountain View, CA: Mayfield.

College Board. (1988). *Guidelines on the uses of College Board test scores and related data.* New York: The College Entrance Examination Board.

Contributors sought. (1990, November). *NASP Communique, 19,* 5.

Cordes, C. (1984, September). Publishers, users discuss quality, use of tests. *APA Monitor, 15,* 14–16.

Costello, S., & Weiss, D. (1984, February). *A summary of guidelines for test users.* ETS Research Report. Princeton, NJ: Educational Testing Service.

Cronbach, L. J. (1990). *Essentials of psychological testing* (5th ed.). New York: Harper Collins.

Educational Testing Service. (1987). *ETS standards for quality and fairness.* Princeton, NJ: Educational Testing Service.

Educational Testing Service. (1988). *Guidelines for proper use of NTE tests.* Princeton, NJ: Author.

Educational Testing Service. (1989). *Guidelines for the use of GRE scores.* Princeton, NJ: Author.

Elmore, P. B., Ekstrom, R. B., & Diamond, E. E. (in press). Counselors' test use practices: Indicators of the adequacy of measurement training. *Measurement and Evaluation in Counseling and Development.*

Examples of test misuse needed. (1991, January). *The Score, 13,* 12.

Eyde, L. D., Green, B., & Jackson, J. H. (1984, July). *Record of test publishers' meeting at APA*. Washington, DC: American Psychological Association.

Eyde, L. D., Moreland, K. L., Robertson, G. J., Primoff, E. S., & Most, R. B. (1988). *Test user qualifications: A data-based approach to promoting good test use*. Issues in Scientific Psychology. Washington, DC: American Psychological Association.

Eyde, L. D., & Primoff, E. S. (1992). Responsible test use. In M. Zeidner & R. Most (Eds.), *Psychological testing: An inside view* (pp. 441–459). Palo Alto: Consulting Psychologists Press.

Eyde, L. D., & Quaintance, M. K. (1988). Ethical issues and cases in the practice of personnel psychology. *Professional psychology: Research and practice, 19,* 148–154.

Flanagan, J. C. (1954). The critical incident technique. *Psychological Bulletin, 51,* 327–358.

Fremer, J., Diamond, E. E., & Camara, W. J. (1989). Developing a Code of Fair Testing Practices in Education. *American Psychologist, 44,* 1062–1067.

Fruchter, D. A. (1985). Wesman Personnel Classification Test. In D. J. Keyser & R. C. Sweetland (Eds.), *Test Critiques* (Vol. III). Kansas City: Test Corporation of America.

Jenkinson, J. (1991). Restrictions on the use of psychological tests: Who should use what? *Australian Psychologist, 26,* 19–24.

Joint Committee on Testing Practices (1988). *Code of fair testing practices in education*. Washington, DC: Author.

Lambert, N. M. (1991). The crisis in measurement literacy in psychology and education. *Educational Psychologist, 26,* 23–35.

Lowman, R. L. (Ed.). (1985). *Casebook on ethics and standards for the practice of psychology in organizations*. College Park, MD: Society for Industrial and Organizational Psychology, Inc. and Division 14 of the American Psychological Association.

Mehrens, W. A., & Lehmann, I. J. (1985). Testing the test: Interpreting test scores to clients: What score should one use? *Journal of Counseling and Development, 63,* 317–320.

National Association of School Psychologists. (1992a). *Principles for professional ethics*. Silver Spring, MD: Author.

National Association of School Psychologists. (1992b). *Standards for the provision of school psychological services*. Silver Spring, MD: Author.

National Commission on Testing and Public Policy. (1990). *From gatekeeper to gateway: Transforming testing in America*. Chestnut Hill, MA: Author.

Nester, M. A. (1984). Employment testing for handicapped people. *Public Personnel Management, 13,* 417–434.

Office of Ethnic Minority Affairs. (1990). *Guidelines for providers of psychological services to ethnic, linguistic, and culturally diverse populations*. Washington, DC: American Psychological Association.

Pennock-Román, M. (1988). [Review of Differential Aptitude Tests]. In J. T. Kapes & M. M. Mastie (Eds.), *A counselors' guide to career assessment instruments*. Alexandria, VA: National Career Development Association and American Association for Counseling and Development.

Primoff, E. S. (1975). *How to prepare and conduct job element examinations* (Technical Study 75–1). Washington, DC: U.S. Civil Service Commission, Personnel Research and Development Center. (NTIS No. PB 84–148 163)

Primoff, E. S., & Eyde, L. D. (1988). Job element analysis. In S. Gael (Ed.), *The job analysis handbook for business, industry, and government* (Vol. II). (pp. 807–824). New York: Wiley.

Rawlins, M. E., & Eberly, C. G. (1991). Infusing counseling skills in test interpretation. *Journal of Counselor Education and Supervision, 31,* 109–120.

Robertson, G. J. (1992). Psychological tests: Development, publication, and distribution. In M. Zeidner & R. Most (Eds.), *Psychological testing: An inside view* (pp. 159–214). Palo Alto, CA: Consulting Psychologists Press.

Society for Industrial and Organizational Psychology, Inc. (1987). *Principles for the validation and use of personnel selection procedures* (3rd ed.). College Park, MD: Author.

Standards for educational and psychological testing. (1985). Washington, DC: American Psychological Association.

Test misuse: A target of concern. (1990, August). *ASHA, 32,* 10.

Test User Training Work Group formed. (1990, January). *The Score, 12,* 16.

Test User Training Work Group needs examples of test misuse. (1991, January). The *Industrial–Organizational Psychologist, 28,* 119–120.

Thorndike, R. M., Cunningham, G. K., Thorndike, R. L., & Hagen, E. P. (1991). *Measurement and evaluation in psychology and education* (5th ed.). New York: Macmillan.

Tinsley, H. E. A., & Bradley, R. W. (1986). Testing the test: Test interpretation. *Journal of Counseling and Development, 64,* 462–466.

INDEX